ESL TEACHER'S BOOK OF INSTANT
WORD GAMES
for Grades 7-12

W9-AXF-822

HELENE D. HUTCHINSON

Illustrations by Yelina Noskina

DISCARD
BETHANY
COLLEGE
LIBRARY

**THE CENTER FOR APPLIED
RESEARCH IN EDUCATION**
West Nyack, New York 10994

Library of Congress Cataloging-Publication Data

Hutchinson, Helene D.
    ESL teacher's book of instant word games for grades 7-12 / Helene
Hutchinson : illustrations by Yelina Noskina.
        p. cm.
    ISBN 0-87628-132-3 (pbk.). —ISBN 0-87628-270-2 (spiral)
    1. English language—Study and teaching (Secondary)—Foreign
speakers—Simulation methods. 2. Word games. I. Title.
PE1128.A2H87   1997   97-3228
428'.0071'2—dc21   CIP

© 1997 by The Center for Applied Research in Education

All rights reserved. Permission is given for individual ESL teachers to reproduce the worksheets for classroom use. Reproduction of these materials for an entire school system is strictly forbidden.

Printed in the United States of America

10 9 8 7 6 5 4 3 2 1   10 9 8 7 6 5 4 3 2 1

ISBN 0-87628-132-3 (pbk.)   0-87628-270-2 (spiral)

ATTENTION: CORPORATIONS AND SCHOOLS

Prentice Hall books are available at quantity discounts with bulk purchase for educational, business, or sales promotional use. For information, please write to: Prentice Hall Career & Personal Development Special Sales, 240 Frisch Court, Paramus, NJ 07652. Please supply: title of book, ISBN, quantity, how the book will be used, date needed.

PRENTICE HALL
Career & Personal Development
Paramus, NJ 07652
A Simon & Schuster Company

On the World Wide Web at http://www.phdirect.com

Prentice Hall International (UK) Limited, *London*
Prentice Hall of Australia Pty. Limited, *Sydney*
Prentice Hall Canada, Inc., *Toronto*
Prentice Hall Hispanoamericana, S.A., *Mexico*
Prentice Hall of India Private Limited, *New Delhi*
Prentice Hall of Japan, Inc., *Tokyo*
Simon & Schuster Asia Pte. Ltd., *Singapore*
Editora Prentice Hall do Brasil, Ltda., *Rio de Janeiro*

DEDICATION

To my editor, Connie Kallback, who believed I could do this book
and helped to frame it.

ACKNOWLEDGMENTS

I want to thank William Hutchinson for his tireless proofreading of the manuscript and my old friend, William Terrel, for editorial assistance. I am particularly grateful to my editor, Connie Kallback, for her ready accessibility, warmth, flexibility, and ability to make swift, sure decisions. Above all, I want to thank my students who taught me everything I know about teaching ESL.

ABOUT THE AUTHOR

Helene Hutchinson has taught at all levels from kindergarten through college. She began her career in the Chicago Public Schools, teaching English to the foreign born for the Chicago Board of Education Americanization Division and remedial and accelerated English classes at Du Sable High School. After leaving the High School, she joined the faculty of the Chicago City Community College and later accepted a position at Kendall College in Evanston, Illinois.

Ms. Hutchinson is the author of the Scott Foresman 1970's English textbook bestseller *Mixed Bag* which won state and national awards, traveled around the world on a tour of American graphics, and sold in 51 countries. Subsequent publications include Holt Rinehart, and Winston's *Black Culture: Reading and Writing Black* and Glencoe Press textbooks, *The Hutchinson Guide to Research* and *Horizons: Activities for the Vocational-Technical School English Class.*

Ms. Hutchinson is currently teaching English to Japanese businessmen and their families. Teaching areas include beginning reading, grammar, structure, conversation, social phrases, American idiom and slang, as well as TOEFL and SAT preparation.

ABOUT THE ILLUSTRATOR

Yelina Noskina is a resident of a Chicago suburb, and has her own history with learning English as a second language, having immigrated to the United States from the Ukraine in her childhood. She is at this time pursuing a Ph.D. in the sciences; however, she has never forgotten the desire she had at one time to be an artist. She still tries to get in some "creative" time during her busy school schedule.

ABOUT THIS RESOURCE

ESL Teacher's Book of Instant Word Games for Grades 7-12 is a collection of reproducible, supplemental activities intended to be used whenever and however you want to use them in your ESL classes. The activities are designed to entertain and teach simultaneously, combining language concepts, engaging art, and puzzle solving. Learning actually becomes a pleasant by-product of the assorted word games. The puzzles themselves are not only fun, but self-correcting mechanisms, as the puzzles work only when answers are correct.

You can use these word games in competitions, as warm-ups, or as fillers when your own planned materials take less time than you anticipated. Sometimes, the activities may work as adjuncts to teaching when you want to add related concepts or reinforce those you have already taught. Often explanatory materials precede activities, though you may wish to augment explanations provided on the worksheets.

The book is divided into five sections: *Words and Phrases* (48 activities), *Grammar* (69 activities), *Structure* (40 activities), *Pronunciation* (29 activities), and *Social Phrases* (14 activities). *Words and Phrases* contains not only useful vocabulary relating to money, careers, sports, and other areas, but also homonyms, antonyms, synonyms, idioms, and slang. Idioms and slang are often vitally important to the newcomer who is trying to make American friends and comprehend a different culture. The sections *Grammar* and *Structure* give students practice in basic English organization. *Pronunciation* introduces newcomers to sound distinctions that might not occur in their native languages. *Social Phrases,* sometimes best taught to intermediate and advanced students only, offers standard expressions that occur in social exchanges.

Words and Phrases and *Grammar* introduce many expressions that native speakers know intuitively, but that must be learned consciously and often laboriously by speakers of English as a second language. These expressions include verbal idioms such as *break in, break out, break up,* and *break down;* verbal oddities like *I'm washing up* (not down); and slang like *the car's a lemon* (not an orange). In *Grammar,* students also learn about count and non-count nouns that native speakers use intuitively and ESL students find baffling. Native speakers, for example, no matter how ungrammatical, will never talk about having many money and too much pennies. In essence the activities in this book have been developed to meet the specific needs of your ESL students, even though some of the activities will also work in regular English classes.

The word games in the individual sections are sequentially arranged in terms of graduated levels of difficulty and labeled beginning, intermediate, and advanced. Though there is a general progression from less difficult to more difficult, the designations are really only advisory as, of course, only you know what's suitable for your students. *Structure* has only two beginning activities because the word games that follow presuppose familiarity with verb tenses often not taught until intermediate ESL. However, *your* beginning students may be able to use easier activities that are labeled intermediate. A special feature of this book is the complete answer key at the back of the book.

With your basic program, familiarity with your students' needs, and these supplemental activities, you can help your ESL students combine pleasure and language development. You can lead them on a joyous journey of discovery. Bon voyage!

Helene Hutchinson

CONTENTS

SECTION ONE
WORDS AND PHRASES • 1

Beginning ESL

Intermediate ESL

Advanced ESL

SECTION TWO
GRAMMAR • 63

Beginning ESL

Intermediate ESL

Advanced ESL

SECTION THREE
STRUCTURE • 141

Beginning ESL

Intermediate ESL

Advanced ESL

SECTION FOUR
PRONUNCIATION • 189

Intermediate ESL

Advanced ESL

SECTION FIVE
SOCIAL PHRASES • 221

Beginning ESL

Intermediate ESL

Advanced ESL

ANSWER KEY • 239

SECTION ONE

WORDS
AND
PHRASES

1-1   GIVE ME A HAND: BODY PARTS

This is a drawing of Ho Buom from Korea. Put the parts of his body in the crossword puzzle. *A* = across. *D* = down.

LIST OF BODY PARTS

Arm
Ankle
Biceps
Calf
Chest
Ears
Elbow
Eyebrow
Foot
Forehead
Hair
Hand
Knee
Leg
Mouth
Neck
Nose
Palm
Shoulders
Teeth
Thigh
Thumb
Wrist

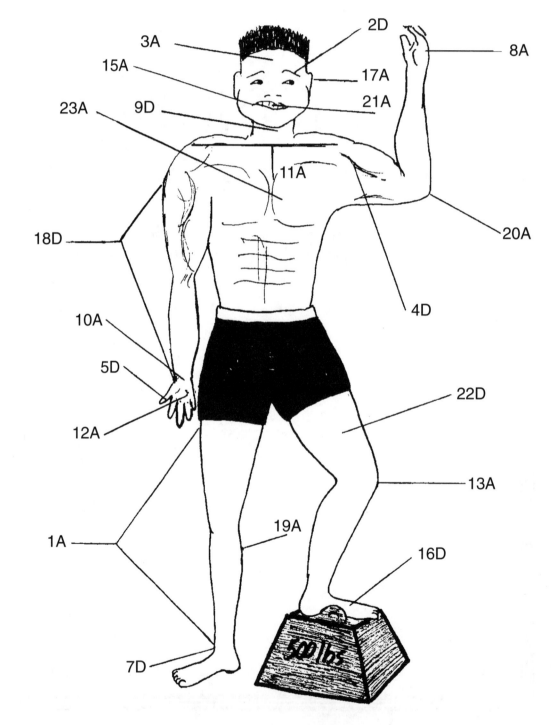

© 1997 by The Center for Applied Research in Education

1-1 Give Me a Hand: Body Parts (*Continued*)

© 1997 by The Center for Applied Research in Education

1-2   APPEARANCES COUNT: CLOTHING WORDS

1. What clothes are on the bed in Slim's room?

2. What clothes are on the floor in Slim's room?

3. What is Slim wearing?

4. Which items in Slim's room come in pairs?

Write your answers on the back of this sheet.

© 1997 by The Center for Applied Research in Education

5. What clothes are on the bed in Stacy's room?

6. What clothes are on the floor in Stacy's room?

7. What is hanging on the door in Stacy's room?

8. What clothes are in the closet in Stacy's room?

9. What is on the chair in Stacy's room?

10. What items in Stacy's room come in pairs?

Write your answers on the back of this sheet.

© 1997 by The Center for Applied Research in Education

BONUS QUESTION: What is the meaning of "appearances count"?

Beginning ESL

1-3   HOW'S THE WEATHER?: WEATHER WORDS

Read the list of weather words below. Put numbers of pictures on the back of this page. Write the correct words under each number.

1. Breezy
2. Calm
3. Chilly
4. Clear
5. Cold
6. Cool
7. Damp
8. Dry
9. Freezing
10. Frigid
11. Hot
12. Humid
13. Icy
14. Mild
15. Moist
16. Sunny
17. Warm
18. Windy
19. Spring
20. Summer
21. Fall or Autumn
22. Winter

1.

2.

3.

4.

© 1997 by The Center for Applied Research in Education

Name_____   Date_____

1-4   WORLD OF NATURE: BIRDS AND BEES

Write the name of each animal in the blanks. The animals are pictured. One letter is provided for each animal's name. The first letters of the animals' names will spell the name of a large animal. Number 1 is done for you.

1.   _ _ _ _ _ E   (<u>H</u> <u>O</u> <u>R</u> <u>S</u> <u>E</u>)

2.   _ _ _ E _ _ _ _ _

3.   _ _ _ _ _ _ _ _ E _

4.   _ I _ _

5.   _ _ _ _ _ I _ _ _

6.   _ _ _ O _ _ _

7.   O _ _ _

8.   _ _ E _ _

9.   _ _ _ E _ _ _ _ _

10. _ _ _ _ E _

11. _ I _ _ _ _ _ _

12. _ _ _ _ _ E _ _ _ _

1.

2.

3.

4.

5.

6.

7.

8.

9.

10.

11.

12.

© 1997 by The Center for Applied Research in Education

Beginning ESL

1-5   YUM, YUM: FOOD AND DRINK

Try to unscramble the food words below and work the foods puzzle by placing the words from the list in the grid.

SCRAMBLED WORDS

Beverages

1. FOCEEF   __ __ __ __ __ __

2. COEK   __ __ __ __

Dairy Products

3. MAREC   __ __ __ __ __

4. SEEECH   __ __ __ __ __ __

Fish

5. NUTA   __ __ __ __

6. NOMALS   __ __ __ __ __ __

Fruit

7. NNAAAB   __ __ __ __ __ __

8. WIIK   __ __ __ __

Grains and Foods Using Flour

9. DABER   __ __ __ __ __

10. NORCLEAM   __ __ __ __ __ __ __ __

Meat

11. EBFE   __ __ __ __

12. OKPR   __ __ __ __

Poultry

13. KDCU   __ __ __ __

© 1997 by The Center for Applied Research in Education

Seasonings and Condiments

14. TLSA

__ __ __ __

15. SUMRDTA

__ __ __ __ __ __ __

Shellfish

16. BRAC

__ __ __ __

17. PIMRHS

__ __ __ __ __ __

Vegetables

18. SRTORAC

__ __ __ __ __ __ __

19. SPAE

__ __ __ __

20. RNCO

__ __ __ __

PUZZLE WORD LIST

Across

carrots
coke
ham
peach
peas
salt
tuna

Down

apples
corn
crab
eggs
meat
onions
peas
radishes
spinach
tea

© 1997 by The Center for Applied Research in Education

Beginning ESL

1-6   PARDON ME, DO YOU HAVE THE TIME?: TELLING TIME

Match each clock with the time on the left by putting the clock letters beside the times. Then transfer the letters to the numbered blanks below the directions. If your answers are correct, you will make a palindrome. A palindrome reads the same backward and forward.

W __ __   __ __   __   __ __ __   __   __ __ __
1   2   3   4   5   6   7   8   9   10   11 12 13

1. Five minutes after three _____W_____

2. Three forty-five _____

3. Three-thirty _____

4. Three twenty-five _____

5. Twenty to five _____

6. Fifteen to four _____

7. Five to one _____

8. A quarter to four _____

9. Four-forty _____

10. Twenty-five minutes after three _____

11. Half past three _____

12. 3:45 _____

13. 3:05 _____

A

B

C

D

E

I

R

S

T

W

© 1997 by The Center for Applied Research in Education

1-7 SHAPE UP: SHAPES AND LINES

Match each shape with the word for the shape. Put the correct number in the blank beside the description. Then shade each number in the design square below. The unshaded numbers will give you a new shape.

A. Circle _____23_____
B. Wide oval _____12_____
C. Narrow oval _____
D. Square _____
E. Rectangle _____
F. Triangle _____
G. Cone _____
H. Grid _____
I. Crescent _____
J. Zigzag _____
K. Diamond _____
L. Arch _____
M. Heart _____
N. Star _____
O. Arrow _____
P. Perpendicular _____
Q. Horizontal line _____
R. Check _____
S. Diagonal line _____
T. Cross _____
U. Parallel lines _____
V. Vertical line _____

© 1997 by The Center for Applied Research in Education

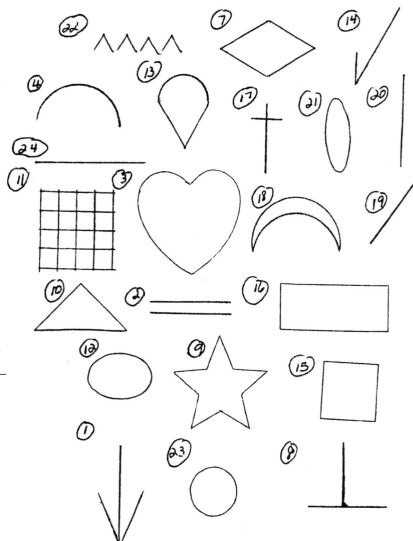

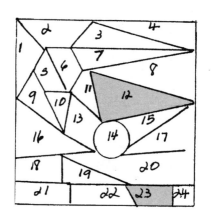

1-8 DAY BEFORE YESTERDAY: TIME EXPRESSIONS

Use the calendar to answer the questions. Write your answer on the blank line following each question. Several are done for you.

Sunday	Monday	Tuesday	Wednesday	Thursday	Friday	Saturday
1	2	3	4	5	6	7
8	9	10	11	12	13	14
15	16	17	18	19	20	21
22	23	24	25	26	27	28
29	30	31			**January**	

Today is Wednesday the 11th.

1. What day was yesterday? <u>Yesterday was Tuesday the 10th.</u>

2. What day was the day before yesterday? _____

_____

3. What day is tomorrow? _____

4. What day is the day after tomorrow? _____

_____

5. What date is next Wednesday? <u>Next Wednesday is the 18th.</u>

6. What date is Wednesday after next? _____

_____

7. What date was last Wednesday? _____

8. What date was Wednesday before last? <u>Wednesday before last was December the 28th.</u>

© 1997 by The Center for Applied Research in Education

1-8   Day Before Yesterday: Time Expressions *(Continued)*

9. What month was last month? _____

10. What month was the month before last? _____

11. What month is next month? _____

12. What did Slim do last night?   Last night, Slim went ice skating with Stacy.

13. What did you do last night? _____

_____

14. What did you do yesterday morning? _____

_____

15. What did you do yesterday afternoon? _____

_____

16. What did you do last Saturday? _____

_____

17. What did you do Saturday before last? _____

_____

18. What did you do last summer? _____

19. What are you going to do tomorrow morning?   Tomorrow morning, I'm going to go to school.

20. What are you going to do tomorrow afternoon? _____

21. What are you going to do tomorrow night? _____

22. What are you going to do next Saturday? _____

23. What are you going to do next summer? _____

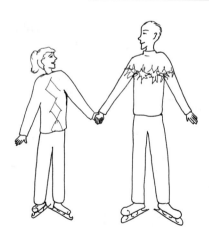

Last night, Slim went
ice skating with Stacy.

© 1997 by The Center for Applied Research in Education

1-9   HE'S WORTH A MILLION BUCKS: MONEY WORDS

Put the numbers of the correct answers in the blanks after the questions. When the numbers have been filled in, trace lines connecting them on the dot picture below. Be sure to follow the order in which the numbers occur in the blanks. The first three answers have been entered for you and traced on the dot picture. Begin your tracing with the number answer for question D.

A. What are five pennies?   __11__
B. What are ten pennies
    or two nickels?   __16__
C. What are "two bits" or
    twenty-five pennies   __25__
    or five nickels?
D. What are fifty pennies
    or ten nickels or two
    quarters or five
    dimes?   _____
E. What is a buck or
    one hundred pennies
    or ten dimes or four
    quarters or twenty
    nickels?   _____
F. What is a C note?   _____
G. What is a grand?   _____
H. What is a fin?   _____
I. What are bills?   _____
J. What are one thousand
    thousand-dollar bills?   _____
K. What is a thousand
    million?   _____
L. What is a trillion?   _____
M. What is a five spot?   _____
N. What is a zillion?   _____
O. What is a cent?   _____

1. A penny
2. A dollar
3. A million dollars
4. Fourteen cents
5. One thousand dollars
6. A number with twelve zeros
7. A number with five zeros
8. A half-dollar
9. Five dollars
10. Forty-five dollars
11. A nickel
12. Paper money
13. Two thousand dollars
14. A billion dollars
15. A number with fifteen zeros
16. A dime
17. A half-penny
18. One bit
19. One hundred dollars
20. Thirty-five cents
21. A very large amount of money;
    not a real number
22. Twelve dollars
23. Ten dollars
24. Twelve nickels
25. A quarter

© 1997 by The Center for Applied Research in Education

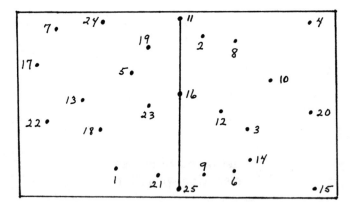

1-10   BINGO: SPORTS AND RECREATIONS

Put the names of the sports and games in the correct boxes in the grid. If your answers are right, you will spell the activity in picture number 7 in the shaded vertical spaces.

1.

2.

3.

4.

5.

6.

7.

7.

1.

2.

3.

4.

5.

6.

© 1997 by The Center for Applied Research in Education

1-11 SILVER BLADES: SPORTS AND RECREATIONS

Can you fit the names of each of these sports and recreations into the grid? Each one has an *I* in it. The final one or two letters are given.

1.

2.

3.

4.

5.

6.

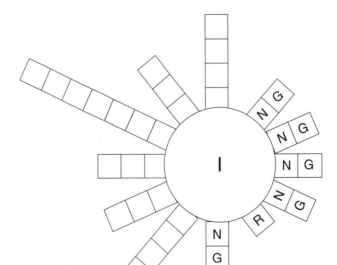

© 1997 by The Center for Applied Research in Education

© 1997 by The Center for Applied Research in Education

Name_____   Date_____

1-12 IT'S A HOMER: SPORTS AND RECREATIONS

Can you fit the names of the sports and games into the puzzle grid? Word lengths and clue letters will help you.

1.

2.

3.

4.

5.

6.

| A | R | C | H | E | R | Y |

| | | W | | | |

| C | A | | | | | |

1-13 WORD SEARCH: MORE SPORTS
AND RECREATIONS

Can you find the names of the six sports pictured? Four are found from left to right; one, from top to bottom; and one, diagonal.

1.

2.

3.

4.

5.

6.

M	A	N	H	O	M	E	R	U	N	G	O	L
M	E	T	O	B	O	G	G	A	N	I	N	G
H	E	S	C	F	O	O	T	B	A	L	L	I
B	A	S	K	E	T	B	A	L	L	Y	O	U
H	I	U	E	Y	C	A	N	O	E	I	N	G
I	T	R	Y	O	D	A	R	C	H	E	R	Y
N	O	F	Y	E	S	I	R	I	D	I	N	G
O	H	I	C	A	R	D	V	J	A	Z	Z	O
U	S	N	T	R	A	C	K	I	B	A	L	L
U	P	G	B	O	X	I	N	G	N	O	F	F
W	A	T	E	R	S	K	I	I	N	G	O	X

© 1997 by The Center for Applied Research in Education

Name_____ Date_____

1-14   NO LEFT TURN: ROAD SIGNS

Put the letter of each road sign in the blank beside the correct meaning.

A.

B.

C.

D.

E.

I.

J.

K.

L.

M.

___E___ 1. Winding Road

_____ 2. No Entry

_____ 3. Road Work

_____ 4. Merging Traffic

_____ 5. No Left Turn

_____ 6. Deer Crossing

_____ 7. No U Turn

_____ 8. Right Turn

_____ 9. Stop

_____ 10. Slippery Road

_____ 11. Hill

_____ 12. Yield

_____ 13. Pedestrian Crossing

_____ 14. One Way

_____ 15. Divided Highway

_____ 16. Cross Road

_____ 17. No Parking

_____ 18. Signal Ahead

_____ 19. Railroad Crossing

F.

G.

H.

N.

O.

P.

Q.

R.

S.

© 1997 by The Center for Applied Research in Education

1-14   Vocabulary Review for No Left Turn: Road Signs (*Continued*)

Underline the correct answers.

1. A pedestrian is
   A. a person walking.
   B. an animal crossing the road.
   C. a vehicle.

2. A winding road
   A. curves again and again.
   B. goes straight.
   C. goes uphill.

3. No entry means
   A. you must turn right.
   B. you can go in.
   C. you can't go in.

4. Road work ahead means
   A. road workers are needed.
   B. factory ahead.
   C. construction ahead.

5. Merging traffic
   A. goes northeast and northwest or southeast and southwest.
   B. comes together.
   C. goes in opposite directions.

6. Deer are
   A. pedestrians.
   B. animals.
   C. road workers.

7. Hills are
   A. roadblocks.
   B. small mountains.
   C. signals.

8. Slippery means
   A. icy or wet.
   B. rocky.
   C. steep.

9. A signal is
   A. a crossroad.
   B. a traffic light.
   C. a bridge.

10. If you yield to another car,
    A. you go first.
    B. you make a U turn.
    C. you let that car go first.

© 1997 by The Center for Applied Research in Education

1-15 COUNT ME IN: NUMBERS

January

Sun.	Mon.	Tue.	Wed.	Thur.	Fri.	Sat.
1	2	3	4	5	6	7
8	9	10	11	12	13	14
15	16	17	18	19	20	21
22	23	24	25	26	27	28
29	30	31				

Part 1.

Write the days of the month in words and in ordinal numbers (1st, 2nd, etc.).

January	1	First	1st		10	_____	_____
	2	Second	2nd		11	_____	_____
	3	Third	3rd		20	Twentieth	_____
	4	Fourth	4th		21	Twenty-first	_____
	5	Fifth	5th		22	_____	_____
	6	_____	_____		23	_____	_____
	7	_____	_____		30	Thirtieth	_____
	8	_____	_____		31	_____	_____
	9	Ninth	_____				

Part 2.

Fill in the blanks with words for the following numbers.

11	Eleven		47	_____
12	Twelve		50	Fifty
13	Thirteen		51	_____
14	Fourteen		52	_____
15	Fifteen		60	Sixty
16	_____		65	_____
17	_____		70	Seventy
20	Twenty		78	_____
21	_____		80	Eighty
22	_____		86	_____
23	_____		90	Ninety
30	Thirty		99	_____
31	_____		100	One hundred
32	_____		101	One hundred one
40	Forty		109	_____
41	_____		110	One hundred ten
			119	_____
			155	_____

© 1997 by The Center for Applied Research in Education

Name_____ Date_____

1-16 THE BUTCHER, THE BAKER, THE CANDLESTICK MAKER: JOBS AND PROFESSIONS

In the blanks under each picture, copy the number beside the correct job title. Then, look at the list of job descriptions and put the correct letter next to each job title. The first one is done for you.

Job titles

1. Police officer
2. Firefighter
3. Painter
4. Mail carrier
5. Salesperson
6. Doctor

Job descriptions

A. This person will save you from a burning building.
B. This person brings letters.
C. This person cares for the sick.
D. This person arrests criminals.
E. This person might work at a large department store.
F. This person changes the color of your walls.

1.

_____4_____ _____B_____

4.

_____ _____

2.

_____ _____

5.

_____ _____

3.

_____ _____

6.

_____ _____

© 1997 by The Center for Applied Research in Education

1-17 · YES, YOUR HONOR: MORE JOBS AND PROFESSIONS

In the blanks under each picture, copy the number beside the correct job title. Then, look at the list of job descriptions and put the correct letter next to each title number.

Job titles

1. Judge
2. Chef
3. Dentist
4. Food server
5. Veterinarian

Job descriptions

A. This person takes care of sick animals.
B. This person cleans your teeth.
C. This person brings you your food in a restaurant.
D. This person cooks food in a restaurant.
E. This person tells criminals how long they must stay in jail.

1.

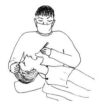

_____ _____

4.

_____ _____

2.

_____ _____

5.

_____ _____

3.

_____ _____

© 1997 by The Center for Applied Research in Education

1-18 LEAKY PIPE: STILL MORE JOBS AND PROFESSIONS

In the blanks under each picture, copy the number beside the correct job title. Then, look at the list of job descriptions and put the correct letter next to each title number.

Job titles

1. Plumber
2. Scientist
3. Secretary
4. Carpenter
5. Artist

Job descriptions

A. This person can build a bookcase.
B. This person can fix your toilet.
C. This person paints pictures.
D. This person types letters in an office.
E. This person does experiments in a laboratory.

1.

_____ _____

2.

_____ _____

3.

_____ _____

4.

_____ _____

5.

_____ _____

© 1997 by The Center for Applied Research in Education

Name _____   Date _____

1-19   MOON WALK: MORE CAREER CHOICES

In the blanks under each picture, copy the number beside the correct job title. Then, look at the list of job descriptions and put the correct letter next to each job title.

Job titles

1. Photographer
2. Astronaut
3. Nurse
4. Bank teller
5. Teacher

Job descriptions

A. This person takes your money and gives you money.
B. This person stands in front of a classroom.
C. This person takes pictures with a camera.
D. This person travels in outer space.
E. This person takes care of sick people.

1.
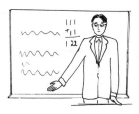
_____ _____

4.

_____ _____

2.

_____ _____

5.

_____ _____

3.

_____ _____

© 1997 by The Center for Applied Research in Education

1-20 ALL IN THE FAMILY: FAMILY WORDS

Put the letter of each family word in the correct blank.

A Mother	F. Niece	K. Mother-in-law	P. Husband
B. Father	G. Grandmother	L. Father-in-law	Q. Son
C. Aunt	H. Grandfather	M. Daughter-in-law	R. Daughter
D. Uncle	I. Great-grandmother	N. Son-in-law	S. Cousin
E. Nephew	J. Great-grandfather	O. Wife	

1. The man a woman marries is her ___P_____.

2. The man your mother married is your _____.

3. A female is her mother's and father's _____.

4. Your mother's or father's mother is your _____.

5. Your mother's or father's grandfather is your _____.

6. Your wife's mother is your _____.

7. Your son's wife is your _____.

8. A male is his mother's and father's _____.

9. The woman your father married is your _____.

10. Your mother's or father's grandmother is your _____.

11. Your mother's or father's father is your _____.

12. Your father's or mother's sister is your_____.

13. Your sister's or brother's daughter is your _____.

14. Your father's or mother's brother is your _____.

15. The woman a man marries is his _____.

16. Your daughter's husband is your _____.

17. Your aunt's and uncle's son or daughter is your _____.

18. Your wife's father is your _____.

19. Your brother's or sister's son is your _____.

© 1997 by The Center for Applied Research in Education

1-21   MAP RAP: GEOGRAPHY WORDS

First, study the definitions. Second, match the questions and answers below the definitions. Use the map provided to do this. Put the *number* of the correct answer in the first blank beside the question. Put the *letter* following the answer in the second blank beside the question. Third, transfer the *letters* to the numbered blanks immediately below. The first one is done for you. If your answers are correct, you will spell the name of a large, cold body of land.

A
___   ___   ___   ___   ___   ___   ___   ___   ___   ___
1   2   3   4   5   6   7   8   9   10

Definitions

- **Longitude:**   Lines on a map that run north and south from the North Pole to the South Pole.

- **Meridians:**   Lines of longitude are also called meridians.

- **Latitude:**   Lines of latitude run east and west around the globe.

- **Parallels:**   Lines of latitude are also called parallels.

- **Degrees:**   Measurements of longitude and latitude are each 1/360 of a circle.

- **Equator:**   The east–west line around the globe. It is at 0 degrees latitude.

- **Prime meridian:** The north–south line around the globe. It is at 0 degrees longitude.

- **Coordinates:**   The points where lines of longitude and latitude meet.

- **Hemisphere:**   One half of a sphere. The equator divides the Earth into the northern and southern hemispheres. The prime meridian divides the Earth into the eastern and western hemispheres.

- **Scale:**   *Examples:* 1/2 inch on the map equals 100 miles. 1 inch on the map equals 200 miles.

© 1997 by The Center for Applied Research in Education

1-21 Map Rap: Geography Words (*Continued*)

Questions

1. What longitude is San Francisco?   <u>12</u>   <u>A</u>

2. What latitude is San Francisco?   __   __

3. What are the nearest coordinates for Cape Town, South Africa?   __   __

4. Is Africa in the northern hemisphere, the southern hemisphere, or in both?   __   __

5. What parallel shown on the map is San Francisco nearest to?   __   __

6. What meridian shown on the map is Lima, Peru nearest to?   __   __

7. What continent is both on the equator and on the prime meridian?   __   __

8. On the map's scale, how many miles does one inch equal?   __   __

9. On the map's scale, how many miles would 2 1/2 inches equal?   __   __

10. Is Sydney, Australia in the eastern or western hemisphere?   __   __

Answers

1. It is in the northern *and* southern hemispheres. (A)

2. It is in the eastern and western hemispheres. (D)

3. It is in the northern and eastern hemispheres. (F)

4. 38 degrees (N)

5. 98 degrees (P)

6. 138 degrees (M)

7. 20 degrees longitude, about 36 degrees latitude (T)

8. 14 degrees longitude, about 170 degrees latitude (Q)

9. 40 degrees longitude, about 40 degrees latitude (Y)

10. Eastern (A)

11. Western (S)

12. 120 (A)

13. 150 (Z)

14. 1,600 (I)

15. 500 (W)

16. 250 (U)

17. 40 degrees (R)

18. 170 degrees (H)

19. 4,000 (C)

20. 3,000 (K)

21. Africa (T)

22. North America (Z)

23. South America (J)

24. Asia (G)

25. 80 degrees (C)

26. 135 degrees (X)

27. 190 degrees (V)

© 1997 by The Center for Applied Research in Education

© 1997 by The Center for Applied Research in Education

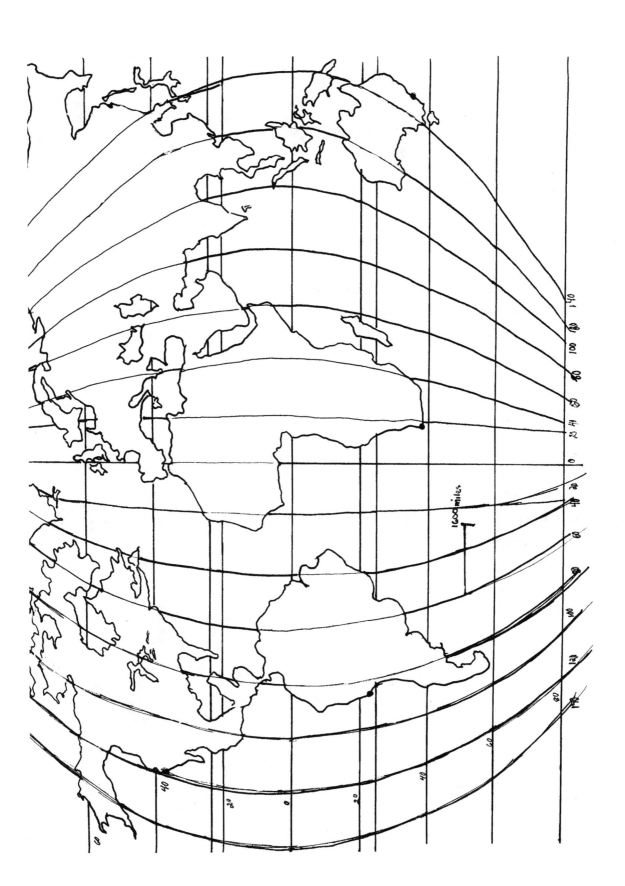

1-22   DOUBLE TROUBLE: HOMONYMS

The words on the right below have more than one meaning. Put the number of each word next to the correct pair of definitions on the left. Then place the circled letter beside the word number. If your answers are correct, the letters will spell the answer to the following riddle: WHAT WOULD AMERICA BE CALLED IF EVERYONE HAD PINK CARS? The first one is done for you.

1. A nobleman. Something you do with money.   <u>1</u> <u>C</u>

2. A toy. A big dance. ___ ___

3. The noise a dog makes. The outside of

    a tree. ___ ___

4. Someone who likes baseball or other sports.

    Something you need in hot weather. ___ ___

5. Parts of your body. Weapons of war. ___ ___

6. Something used in baseball. A flying

    rodent. (Mice and rats are other

    rodents.) ___ ___

7. Intelligent. A word that describes the

    sun. ___ ___

8. Something the wind does. What you

    receive when someone hits you. ___ ___

9. People standing behind each other.

    Something you draw with a ruler. ___ ___

1. C(ount)
2. B(a)t
3. Br(i)ght
4. L(i)ne
5. Ba(r)k
6. B(l)ow
7. Fa(n)
8. (A)rms
9. B(a)ll

© 1997 by The Center for Applied Research in Education

"You bore me," said the tree to the woodpecker.

BONUS QUESTION: What are two meanings of *bore*?

Name _____   Date _____

1-23   MY ACHING HEAD: MORE HOMONYMS

Homonyms are words that have the same sound and often the same spelling, but different meanings. There are two definitions for each of the homonyms listed below. Place the correct homonyms in the puzzle grid.

Homonyms

Bank	Land	Pop
Bill	Lot	Sap
Firm	Mad	Seal
Fly	Pet	Top
Kind	Plot	Yard

Across

1. A company. Not soft.

5. A dog or cat. To stroke a dog or cat.

8. Three feet. A grassy place in front or in back of a house.

14. A man's name. A statement of money you owe.

18. A stupid person (slang). A sticky liquid from trees.

29. Not cruel. A type or variety.

33. An empty piece of land. Many.

Down

1. An insect. What birds can do.

4. Angry. Insane or crazy.

5. To hit a baseball high in the air. A word for father.

7. A spinning toy. The upper part of something.

14. A place that keeps money. Snow piled up.

17. What airplanes do when they reach the ground. The ground.

18. To close an envelope. A land and water animal.

20. Things that happen in a story. A secret plan for hostile or illegal action.

© 1997 by The Center for Applied Research in Education

31   **Intermediate ESL**

1-24   SLIM ATE EIGHT HAMBURGERS: HOMOPHONES

Homophones are sound-alikes with different spellings and the same pronunciation. Shade the numbers in the grid of sentences with correctly used homophones. If your choices are correct, you will draw a common homophone.

1	2	3
4	5	6
7	8	9
10	11	12
13	14	15
16	17	18
19	20	21

1. "Some things just aren't *fair*," said Tod.

2. Bus *fare* is so expensive, I can't go to the game.

3. However, I'm going to the state *fair* because I have a ride.

4. *There* are many hard things about living in a new country.

5. You meet a lot of different people. *Their* always saying things you don't understand.

6. In gym, the teacher tells you to go here or *there*, and sometimes you don't understand.

7. Li said, "I can't *bear* to see an animal in a cage. Animals should be free."

8. A *bear*, for example, is an animal that should be free.

9. The boy didn't have a hat on his head. His head was *bare*.

10. There was a narrow *bored* across the stream.

11. I was so *bored* during the movie, I fell asleep.

12. The *principle* is the head of the school.

13. What's your principal reason for wanting to go to college?

14. Your ideas about right and wrong are your *principles*.

15. Always begin names with *capital* letters.

16. "Come *here*," said my mother.

17. "Do you *here* me? I'm talking to you."

18. "I *hear* you perfectly well."

19. I think Mr. and Mrs. Sikand are the nicest people in the *whole* world.

20. The mole dug a *hole* in our yard.

21. Did you *break* your foot when you stepped on the *brake*?

© 1997 by The Center for Applied Research in Education

1-25 ANOTHER WAY OF SAYING THIS: SYNONYMS

Synonyms are words with the same meanings. Place the synonyms for the twenty-six words below in the vertical spaces in the grid. Number 1 should be placed in the *A* column, number 2 in the *B* column, and so on. If your answers are correct, you will use each of the letters of the alphabet. The first one is done for you.

1. Unhappy
2. Lovely, pretty
3. Wide
4. Act
5. Argue
6. Frightened
7. Odd, unusual

8. Strike
9. Intelligent
10. Fair
11. Murder
12. Go
13. Nearly
14. Crazy

15. Truthful
16. Dumb
17. Fast
18. Easy-going, pleasant
19. Nervous
20. Skill

21. Unattractive
22. Trip, journey
23. Terrible
24. Blend
25. Neat
26. Blue

© 1997 by The Center for Applied Research in Education

Intermediate ESL

1-26   YOU GOT ME WRONG: ANTONYMS

Antonyms are words that are opposite in meaning. Write the opposite of each word in the grid to the right. One letter is supplied for each of the words. If your answers are correct, the two shaded horizontal words will be antonyms.

1. Good
2. Quiet
3. Always
4. Ordinary
5. Tough
6. Stupid
7. Thin
8. Empty
9. Ugly
10. Wild
11. Sour
12. Seldom
13. Kind
14. Hardworking

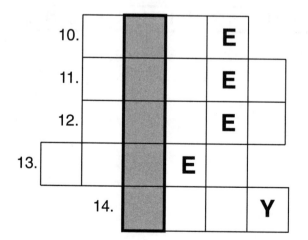

© 1997 by The Center for Applied Research in Education

1-27 THINGS AREN'T WHAT THEY SEEM: IDIOM LITERALIZED

Match the numbered pictures with the correct idioms. There are eight pictures and twelve idioms. Cross out the idioms for which there are no pictures. Put the circled letters in the remaining idioms in the blanks below. Transfer the letters in numerical order. If your answers are right, the circled letters will spell a new idiom that means DO SOMETHING LATER. The first one is done for you.

P
— — — —   — — —   — — — —

© 1997 by The Center for Applied Research in Education

1.

2.

3.

4.

5.

6.

7.

8.

__1__ 1. Pay through the nose	_____ 7. Go Dutch
_____ 2. Crazy	_____ 8. Get in someone's hair
_____ 3. Jump down someone's throat	_____ 9. Hit the hay
_____ 4. Out on a limb	_____ 10. Birds and bees
_____ 5. Pull strings	_____ 11. Cough up
_____ 6. Lemon	_____ 12. Spill the beans

1-28 WHAT DID YOU SAY?: IDIOM AND MEANING

Match the idioms on the left to the definitions on the right. Put the letters of correct definitions in the blanks on the left. Two idioms have the same definition. The letters beside the first fifteen idioms will spell two other idioms that are illustrated on this page.

Idioms

__M__ 1. Pull someone's leg

_____ 2. Jump down someone's throat

_____ 3. Lose face

_____ 4. Pay through the nose

_____ 5. Hit the ceiling

_____ 6. Spill the beans

_____ 7. Hit the hay

_____ 8. A lemon

_____ 9. Out on a limb

_____ 10. Get in someone's hair

_____ 11. Cough up

_____ 12. Smell a rat

_____ 13. Bug someone

_____ 14. Bend over backwards

_____ 15. Blow up

_____ 16. Pull strings

_____ 17. Kick the bucket

_____ 18. Kick up one's heels

_____ 19. Sell for a song

_____ 20. Hit the nail on the head

_____ 21. Birds and bees

_____ 22. Stick to one's guns

_____ 23. Fair weather friend

_____ 24. Go Dutch

_____ 25. Have a ball

_____ 26. Crocodile tears

_____ 27. Off one's rocker

_____ 28. A penny for your thoughts

Definitions

A. Go to sleep

B. Die

C. Use influence

D. Get something exactly right

E. Pay a lot of money for something

F. Give money unwillingly

G. Sell cheaply

H. Try very hard

I. Be suspicious

J. Celebrate

K. In a dangerous position

L. A bad product, often a car

M. Make someone believe a silly story

N. To be embarrassed

O. Speak to another person angrily

P. Someone who is a friend in good times only

Q. Truth about sex

R. Crazy

S. Annoy someone

T. Tell something that is supposed to be secret

U. Please tell me what you're thinking

V. To pay for yourself on a date

W. Pretended grief

X. Have a good time

Y. Get mad

Z. Not give up one's ideas or opinions

BONUS QUESTION: What are the meanings of the two new idioms?

© 1997 by The Center for Applied Research in Education

1-29   A YELLOW BLUEBLOOD: COLOR IDIOM

Read the definitions. Then explain the color idioms below.

Definitions

Black and blue: bruised
Blue: sad
Blue around the gills: sick
Blueblood: an aristocrat
Blue-collar worker: factory
  worker
Goldbrick: avoid work
Grey matter: brains

In the black: out of debt
In the red: in debt
Once in a blue moon: infrequently
Out of the blue: unexpected
Red in the face: embarrassed
White: Caucasian
White as a sheet: frightened
White-collar worker: office worker
Yellow: cowardly

1. A black-and-blue white: A person with bruises _____

2. A blue-collar worker with grey matter: _____

   _____

3. A blue white-collar worker: _____

4. A yellow blueblood: _____

5. I'm in the red once in a blue moon: _____

   _____

6. I was in the black out of the blue: _____

   _____

7. I was red in the face because I was white as a sheet: _____

   _____

8. He goldbricked because he was blue around the gills: _____

   _____

© 1997 by The Center for Applied Research in Education

1-30 IT'S A PIECE OF CAKE: PARTITIVES

Partitives are expressions like "a cup of coffee" or "a loaf of bread." Complete the expressions on the left with appropriate words on the right. Place letters from the right-hand column in the correct blanks on the left. Then transfer these letters to the numbered spaces immediately below these directions. If your answers are correct, you will spell two idioms. The first means something that is very easy. The second means that something happens only once. One of the idioms is illustrated below. The first one is done for you.

```
__        __  __  __  __  __     __  F      __  __  __  __
9         7   2   12  6   12     5   1      6   9   8   12

__        F   __  __  __  __     __  __     __  __  __     __  __  __
9         1   10  9   11  4      2   3      13  4   12     7   9   3
```

1. Ear of _____F_____   A. Cake, pie, meat, wood, cheese
2. Flash of _____   B. Pillow
3. Pat of _____   C. Coffee, tea
4. Ear of _____   D. Sofa
5. Bunch of _____   E. Sand, salt, sugar
6. A cup of _____   F. Corn
7. Gust of _____   G. Plant
8. Slice or loaf of _____ H. Soap
9. Piece of _____   I. Lightning
10. Clap of _____   J. Chairs
11. Drop of _____   K. Bread
12. Grain of _____   L. Thunder
13. Skein of _____   M. Snow
                                 N. Butter
                                 O. Grapes, flowers
                                 P. Wind
                                 Q. Nuts
                                 R. Mail
                                 S. Rain
                                 T. Yarn

© 1997 by The Center for Applied Research in Education

Name _____ **Date** _____

1-31   BLIND AS A BAT: ANIMAL IDIOM

Complete the idiomatic expressions below with the numbers beside the animals on the page. Next transfer the numbers chosen to the cross-shaped grid below. If your answers are correct, the numbers in the cross will total 26 in the horizontal and vertical rows.

A. Blind as a _____1_____

B. Busy as a _____

C. Scaredy _____

D. Dumb as a _____

E. Sly as a _____

F. Big as a _____

G. Brave as a _____

H. Is he a man or a _____

I. Stubborn as a _____

J. Slow as a _____

K. Wise as an _____

L. Dirty as a _____

(4)

(3)

(10)

(12)

(7)

(11)

(2)

(5)

(6)

(8)

(9)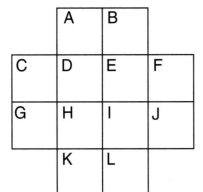

(1)

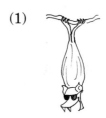

A	B	
C	D	E	F
G	H	I	J
	K	L	

© 1997 by The Center for Applied Research in Education

Intermediate ESL

Name_____   Date_____

1-32 DON'T PUT YOUR FOOT IN YOUR MOUTH: THE PUT FAMILY

Find the suitable idiom for each numbered picture below. Put the number of the picture in the blank after the idiom. Then write the meaning of this idiom on the line below it.

1.    2.    3.    4.

5.    6    7.    8.

A. Put a bee in one's bonnet   __4__

       Get a new idea
_____

B. Put a bug in one's ear   _____

_____

C. Put all one's eggs in one basket   _____

_____

D. Put in one's two cents   _____

_____

E. Put one's foot in one's mouth   _____

_____

F. Put one's nose out of joint   _____

_____

G. Put one's shoulder to the wheel   _____

_____

H. Put our heads together   _____

_____

© 1997 by The Center for Applied Research in Education

1-33 DON'T PULL MY LEG: BODY IDIOM

Put the number of each definition beside the illustrated idioms below.

Definitions

1. Show feelings openly

2. Eager to listen
3. Begin something you want to do
4. Very curious about other people's lives
5. Frighten

6. Trick someone; make someone believe something ridiculous
7. Not have any use for
8. Generous
9. Not look at reality
10. Relax; speak freely

A.

Nosy __4__

B.

Make one's hair stand on end _____

C.

Need something like one needs a hole in the head _____

D.

All ears _____

E.

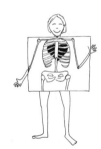

Big hearted _____

F.

Let one's hair down _____

© 1997 by The Center for Applied Research in Education

1-34   IT SMELLS FISHY: FISH IDIOM

Match the definitions and idioms below. Put the circled letters beside the correct idioms. If your choices are correct, you will spell the answer to the riddle below:

What part of Mexico is in Iraq?

Idioms

___T___   1. A cold fish

_____   2. A big fish

_____   3. A big fish in a little pond

_____   4. Neither fish nor fowl

_____   5. Plenty of fish in the sea

_____   6. Drink like a fish

_____   7. Fish for compliments

_____   8. Have other fish to fry

_____   9. A fine kettle of fish

_____   10. Feed the fish

(Neither fish nor fowl)

Definitions

Drown(i)n a river, lake, or ocean

Someon(e)who is important only in a small group

(T)ake too much alcohol

Hav(e)other things to do

A person withou(t)feelings

A confusing affai(r)

Many other peopl(e)suited for a job

Sugges(t)that other people say nice things about you

Th(e) most important person in a group

Not be(l)onging to any group or category

BONUS QUESTION: Explain the title idiom.

© 1997 by The Center for Applied Research in Education

1-35 As I Always Say: Everyday Idioms

What's your IQ (idiom quotient)? Find out by matching everyday idioms and their definitions. Put the letter of the correct definition beside each idiom. Then rank yourself on the scale below.

20–25	correct	170	IQ	Superior
17–19	correct	150	IQ	Excellent
14–16	correct	120	IQ	Above average
11–13	correct	100	IQ	Average
0–13	correct	80	IQ	Below average

Everyday idioms

1. It's about time you showed up. __B__
2. He's afraid of his own shadow. __G__
3. Working around the clock. _____
4. Baker's dozen. _____
5. Stop beating around the bush. _____
6. Cut it out. _____
7. All thumbs. _____
8. My better half. _____
9. Bite the dust. _____
10. Make your blood run cold. _____
11. Boning up on (something). _____
12. Burn the midnight oil. _____
13. Catch 40 winks. _____
14. Give someone the cold shoulder. _____
15. Dead to the world. _____
16. Down in the dumps. _____
17. Drop me a line. _____
18. Get the ax. _____
19. Get wind of something. _____
20. Go fly a kite. _____
21. A good egg. _____
22. In a fog. _____
23. In hot water. _____
24. Has a screw loose. _____
25. Lose your shirt. _____

Definitions

A. Stay up late to play or work
B. You're late
C. Lose a lot of money in business, in the stock market, in gambling
D. Thirteen
E. In trouble
F. Studying; trying to learn a lot about something in a short time
G. Timid
H. Die
I. Working all night and all day, 24 hours
J. Sleep for a short time
K. Sad, gloomy
L. Stop talking indirectly; get to the point
M. Husband or wife; spouse
N. Stop doing that!
O. Horrible
P. Not understanding; confused
Q. Write me a letter or a note
R. Snub someone
S. Go away!
T. Is crazy
U. A good person
V. Hear about
W. Get fired
X. Clumsy
Y. In a deep sleep

(A good egg)

© 1997 by The Center for Applied Research in Education

1-36   FIT AS A FIDDLE: COMMON COMPARISONS

Choose the word from each rhyming group below that will sensibly complete the comparison in the corresponding number.

1. Flock
   Rock
   Knock
   Clock
   Dock
   Sock

2. Ice
   Dice
   Mice
   Advice
   Lice

3. Riddle
   Fiddle
   Diddle
   Piddle

4. Dove
   Above
   Glove

5. Clock
   Sock
   Peacock
   Knock
   Rock

6. Pail
   Mail
   Sail
   Rail
   Hail

7. Fixture
   Picture
   Mixture

8. Bill's
   Hills
   Pills
   Kills
   Fills
   Ills

9. Sold
   Cold
   Gold
   Fold
   Scold
   Rolled

10. Leather
    Feather
    Heather

11. Louse
    House
    Blouse
    Grouse

12. Fail
    Tale
    Doornail
    Mail
    Jail

13. Die
    Pie
    Fly
    Guy
    Sly
    Why

14. Receives
    Thieves
    Grieves
    Deceives

15. Word
    Nerd
    Bird
    Furred
    Occurred

16. Sunny
    Bunny
    Funny
    Money
    Honey

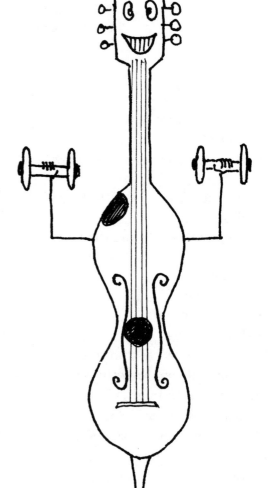

© 1997 by The Center for Applied Research in Education

1-36 Fit as a Fiddle: Common Comparisons *(Continued)*

1. There was a man from Vladivostok
   Who had a head as hard as a _____ rock _____.

2. She wasn't kind, and she wasn't nice.
   She had a heart as cold as _____.

3. He may be thick around the middle,
   But everyone knows he's as fit as a _____.

4. His girlfriend says with pride and love,
   "His clothes just fit him like a _____."

5. Mary Leacock
   Is as proud as a _____.

6. There was a man in the county jail
   Who was sad and tall and thin as a _____.

7. Sweetness and brains—a lovely mixture.
   She is also as pretty as a _____.

8. There was a man named Mr. Wills.
   He was very wise and as old as the _____.

9. There was a man who was strong and bold
   And had a heart as good as _____.

10. We walked one day in the winter weather
    When the fallen snow was as soft as a _____.

11. She was as quiet as a mouse,
    Even though she was as big as a _____.

12. He was white as a sail
    And as dead as a _____.

13. Heavens to Betsy. Me oh my! (Exclamations meaning Oh!)
    Mary Jane is as sweet as _____.

14. The friends walked in the fallen leaves,
    Happy together and thick as _____.

15. "Mother, Mother, have you heard?
    I lost my job, and I'm free as a _____."

16. If only I had a lot of money,
    I'm sure I'd be as sweet as _____.

© 1997 by The Center for Applied Research in Education

1-37 BREAK DOWN THE DOOR: MEANINGS OF BREAK

The meaning of *break* changes when it is followed by different prepositions, such as *in, out, up, down*. Put the correct preposition after *break* in the phrase in parentheses that tells the meaning of each set of sentences. Next, in the box, draw lines between each use of break and the correct preposition. If you draw the lines correctly, they will intersect in the center.

© 1997 by The Center for Applied Research in Education

1. I hate this car. Whenever I'm driving on the highway or going through a busy intersection, something goes wrong. My car stops. I cause a big traffic jam. Other cars start honking.

   (Break <u>down</u>)

2. The thief was very clever. He climbed through a partly open window and found valuable jewelry hidden in a box under a loose floorboard. (Break _____)

3. I don't have smallpox, thank goodness; but my face and arms are covered with small, red spots that itch. (Break _____)

4. My girlfriend and her boyfriend used to love each other. Now they can't stand each other. They are never going to see each other again. (Break _____)

5. The robber was in jail, but he was very clever. When the guard was standing with his back to the cell, the robber silently took the guard's keys. As soon as the guard left, the robber opened the cell door and walked out of the jail through a back exit. (Break _____)

1-37 Break Down the Door: Meanings of Break *(Continued)*

© 1997 by The Center for Applied Research in Education

● BREAK (what a
robber does)

● OUT

DOWN ●

● BREAK (what an
angry couple does)

UP ●

BREAK (what an
● old car does)

BREAK (what a
● rash does)

IN
●

1-38   COME IN, PLEASE: MEANINGS OF COME

The meaning of *come* changes when followed by different prepositions. First, write the name of the word pictured in the blank on the right. Then circle the preposition inside that word. Finally, combine each of the prepositions with *come,* and use each combination in a sentence. The first one is done for you.

1.      P(IN)   Won't you please <u>come in</u>? _____

_____

2.      _____

_____

3.      _____

_____

4.      _____

_____

5.      _____

_____

© 1997 by The Center for Applied Research in Education

1-39 DON'T DO ME IN: MEANINGS OF DO

Fill each blank with the letter of the phrase from the right-hand column that completes the idiom on the left. The first one has been done for you. Three letters are used more than once. If your answers are correct, the letters chosen will give the answer to this riddle:

HOW DO YOU KEEP A SKUNK FROM SMELLING?

The answer to the riddle is illustrated on this page.

© 1997 by The Center for Applied Research in Education

1. kill: do ___H___

2. not have something: do _____

3. need: could do _____

4. cheat someone: do _____

5. end, abolish: do _____

6. have strong will to succeed: do _____

7. improve the appearance of: do _____

8. improve someone's reputation: do _____

9. manage better without something: do _____

10. give money or help to someone: do _____

11. do again: do _____

A. against
B. until
C. behind
D. out of
E. over
F. in front of
G. above
H. away with
I. or die
J. under
K. according to
L. with
M. on
N. credit to
O. without
P. between
Q. after
R. before
S. something for

1-40   Don't Get in Trouble: Meanings of Get

There are many *get* idioms in English. Definitions are on the left. Words that complete each *get* idiom are in the box. Place the correct completing words in the puzzle grid. Some words will be used more than once.

ACROSS

1. Able to move. Get _____.

4. Get injured. Get _____.

6. Become older. Get _____.

7. Leave! Get _____!

8. Rise in the morning. Get _____.

9. Enter a house. Get _____.

11. Grow large. Get _____.

13. Feel ready to eat. Get _____.

15. Do something unpleasant to someone who has treated you badly. Get _____.

18. Scold someone. Get _____.

19. Increase speed. Get _____ speed.

20. Succeed in annoying someone. Get _____.

hungry
hurt
back
about
on
in
up
at
out
big
across
through
to
back
it
nervous

DOWN

1. Make something understood. Get _____.

2. Board a bus. Get _____.

3. Finish work. Get _____.

5. To reach a place. Arrive at. Get _____.

10. Become worried. Get _____.

11. Return. Get _____.

12. Continue work. Get _____ with.

14. Stand. Get _____.

15. Move to the rear. Get _____.

16. Enter a car. Get _____.

17. Understand? Get _____?

18. Board an airplane. Get _____.

© 1997 by The Center for Applied Research in Education

1-40   Don't Get in Trouble: Meanings of Get *(Continued)*

¹A	B	²O	U	³T					
				⁴			⁵		
							⁶		
⁷									
				⁸			⁹	¹⁰	
		¹¹				¹²			
				¹³	¹⁴				
¹⁵									
						¹⁶			
			¹⁷		¹⁸			¹⁹	
		²⁰							

© 1997 by The Center for Applied Research in Education

1-41   I'D LIKE TO TAKE HER OUT: SEPARABLE VERBS

English verbs are often followed by prepositions or adverbs like *take out* or *have on*. Often these prepositions or adverbs can be placed right after the verb *or* after the object. Verbs like this are called separable verbs. Study the verbs, definitions, and models. Next, fill in the blanks in the sentences that follow.

Separable verbs	*Definitions*
have on	wear
kook up	find words in a dictionary
make up	invent
put off	postpone; plan to do later
take out	take someone on a date
try on	put on clothes in a store to see if they fit

Models

Did Katya *have on* her new red dress? *OR*
Did Katya *have* it *on*? *OR*
Did Katya *have* her new red dress *on*?
NOT Did Katya *have on* it?

© 1997 by The Center for Applied Research in Education

1. Did Slim have __on__ his new blue jacket? Yes, he had it __on__.

   He had his new blue jacket __on__.

2. Did Jose look _____ the words in the dictionary? Did he look them _____?
   Yes, he looked the words _____.

3. Did Pedro really see a Martian spacecraft in the schoolyard, or did he make _____ the story? Everyone thinks he made it _____. He often makes stories _____.

4. Slim always puts _____ doing his homework. He put it _____ last night.
   He puts homework _____ so much he might fail the class.

5. Slim wants to take _____ Yuko. He can't because he's going with Stacy. Stacy won't let him take Yuko _____. However, he really wants to take her _____.

6. Lisa tried _____ so many dresses, Marcia got bored waiting. Marcia said, "Please don't try any more dresses _____. I'm tired of watching you try them _____."

1-42   THE ROBBER GOT IN: NON-SEPARABLE VERBS

English verbs are often followed by prepositions or adverbs as in *call on* or *get in*. The parts of non-separable verbs can never be separated. For example, we can say, "I *called on* Mrs. Jones," but not, "I called Mrs. Jones on." Study the verbs, definitions, and models. Then rearrange the words in parentheses to form sentences. The first one is done for you.

Verbs   *Definitions*

call on   visit
get into   enter a car; break into a house
get off   leave a bus, train, or airplane
get on   enter a bus, train, or airplane
get over   recover
look for   try to find
run into   meet

Models

Gregor *ran into* Hans in the hall. *OR*
Gregor *ran into* him in the hall.
NOT Gregor *ran* Hans *into* in the hall.

---

1. (called on/ Rosa/ new neighbors/ her/ Mr. and Mrs. Ramirez)

   Rosa called on her new neighbors, Mr. and Mrs. Ramirez._____

2. (got into/ the empty house/ the robber)

   _____

3. (got off/ from Bombay/ Ranjana and Ashoke/ the airplane)

   _____

4. (got on/ to Minneapolis/ Tadeusz/ the bus)

   _____

5. (got over/ but/ had a cold/ it/ she/ Maria)

   _____

6. (looked for/ Nisme/ ESL book/ find it/ but/ couldn't/ her/ she)

   _____

7. (ran into/ his friend/ Pedro/ in the hall)

   _____

© 1997 by The Center for Applied Research in Education

1-43   I WANT TO TRAVEL, BUT I CAN'T STAND FLYING: VERBS WITH INFINITIVES AND GERUNDS

Some verbs are followed by infinitives, some by gerunds, and others by either infinitives or gerunds. Study the lists and examples below, then answer the questions or complete the sentences below the verb lists. Use the back of this paper if you need more room.

Verbs followed by infinitives

Examples: I *agreed to work* four afternoons a week. Slim *appears to be* happy most of the time.
Wrong: I *agreed working* four afternoons a week.

agree	expect	plan
appear	fail	prepare
arrange	forget	pretend
ask	hope	promise
can afford	intend	refuse
can wait	learn	threaten
decide	need	try
demand	offer	want
deserve		

Verbs followed by gerunds

Examples: The child *admitted* telling a lie.
 Tod *avoided studying* before the test.
Wrong: Tod *avoided to study* before the test.

admit	finish	recommend
appreciate	miss	regret
avoid	postpone	stop
complete	practice	suggest
consider	put off	talk about
discuss	quit	think about
enjoy		

Verbs followed by either infinitives or gerunds: begin, can't stand, continue, like, start.

Examples: Slim *likes sitting* beside Stacy. Slim *likes to sit* beside Stacy.

---

1. Name two things you enjoy doing. I enjoy ice skating and _____swimming_____

2. What do you like to do on weekends? _____

3. What do you like doing at night? _____

4. What do you often put off doing? _____

5. What should smokers stop doing? _____

6. Name three things you can't afford to do. _____

7. What are two things you regret? _____

8. What do you hope to do when you finish high school? _____

9. What did you discuss in class yesterday? _____

10. What do you miss doing in your own country? _____

© 1997 by The Center for Applied Research in Education

1-44   POP THE QUESTION: BOY AND GIRL TALK

In the blanks following each popular slang expression on the left, put the number of the phrase that most clearly defines the expression. Then connect the numbers in the dot-to-dot picture. Follow the numerical order of the answers. If your answers are correct, you will have a picture of a popular activity.

Slang expressions

A. Old flame _20_

B. Blind date ____

C. Fall for ____

D. Play the field ____

E. Go steady with ____

F. Get hitched ____

G. Pop the question ____

H. Fix someone up with ____

I. Break a date ____

J. A knockout ____

K. Nutty about, crazy about ____

L. Lead on ____

M. Pick up ____

N. Give someone the eye ____

O. Broken-hearted ____

P. Macho ____

Q. A jock ____

R. Tall, dark, and handsome ____

S. Honey ____

T. A date ____

U. A tomato ____

V. One-night stand ____

W. Hit on ____

X. Hot ____

Y. Die for ____

Definitions

1. Date only one person

2. A rude word for a girl

3. To like very much at first sight

4. In love with

5. To look at someone

6. Strong and muscular

7. Meet someone without an introduction

8. To get someone to think you like him or her when you don't

9. An athlete

10. Recreational activity with member of opposite sex

11. Introduce someone to a boy or girl

12. Cancel a date

13. Deeply sad because of lost love

14. A way of describing a very good-looking boy

15. A date you are meeting for the first time

16. A way of addressing someone you like or love

17. Get married

18. One date only; a one-night sexual relationship

19. A beautiful girl

20. A boyfriend or girlfriend from the past

21. Ask someone to marry you

22. Date many people

23. Try to make love to someone

24. Very attractive; sexy

25. Want to know very much

© 1997 by The Center for Applied Research in Education

1-44   Pop the Question: Boy and Girl Talk *(Continued)*

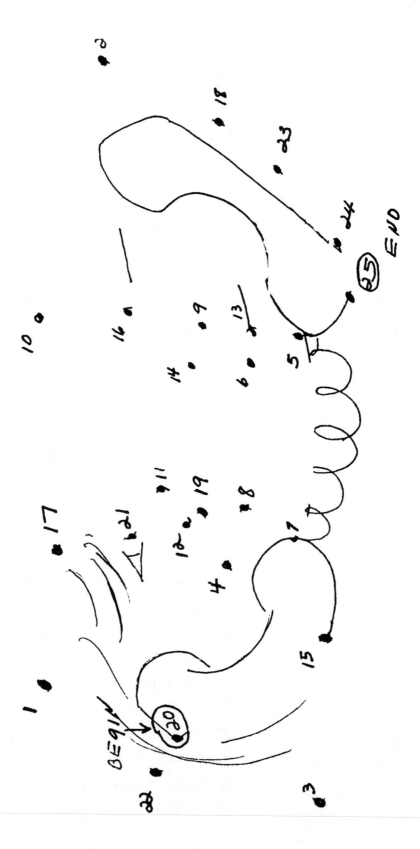

© 1997 by The Center for Applied Research in Education

Name _____   Date _____

1-45   POTPOURRI: MISCELLANEOUS SLANG

Popular American idiomatic and slang expressions are listed in the column to the left. Definitions are listed in the column on the right. Put the numbers of the correct definitions beside the expressions on the left. Then transfer each number to the correct lettered space in the grid below. If your answers are correct, the horizontal, vertical, and diagonal rows of numbers will total 50. (Note that numbered definitions begin with "5" instead of "1.")

Idioms

_20_ A. Broke
_____ B. Loaded
_____ C. Fed up with
_____ D. Clothes horse
_____ E. Sore loser
_____ F. Nest egg
_____ G. Mooch
_____ H. Nitwit
_____ I. Half-baked
_____ J. Bring home the bacon
_____ K. Shape up
_____ L. Brainstorm
_____ M. Cock-and-bull story
_____ N. Nitty gritty
_____ O. Kid around
_____ P. In a jam

Definitions

5. In a difficult situation
6. Having a lot of money
7. Having had too much of something
8. A false story
9. Someone who becomes angry when he or she doesn't win
10. Improve behavior or work quality
11. Earn money for one's family
12. Idiot; stupid person
13. Said of an idea that is not well-thought out
14. Borrow; beg; get something without paying
15. An amount of money that has been saved
16. Discuss; think about; share ideas
17. A woman who loves clothes and wears them well
18. The important part of something
19. Joke with someone
20. Completely without money

(Slim's broke!)

A	B	C	D
E	F	G	H
I	J	K	L
M	N	O	P

57   **Advanced ESL**

© 1997 by The Center for Applied Research in Education

1-46   STONE SOUP: MORE MISCELLANEOUS SLANG

Match the slang idioms in the sentences to the left with the definitions on the right. Put the letter of the correct definition in the blank beside the sentence. When your teacher gives you the correct answers, rate yourself on the Slang Scale below.

Slang Scale	
18–20	You're a brain.
14–17	You're sharp.
10–13	You're not so hot.
0–9	You need to spend more time talking with American friends.

Idioms and slang

Definitions

___H___ 1. When I cleaned the basement, I found a lot of *odds and ends*.

A. Annoyed

B. Extremely happy

_____ 2. My brother is always promising to help me fix the car, but he never does. I'm *fed up with* him.

C. Wished for good luck

D. Avoids work

_____ 3. Whenever John loses a game of chess, he gets mad. He's a real *sorehead*.

E. Unfair treatment

F. A sarcastic and unkind remark

_____ 4. Slim bought himself a *jalopy* for $150.00.

G. Stop

H. Miscellaneous items

_____ 5. Before a test, Khaled is always *on pins and needles*.

I. Easy

J. Very smart

_____ 6. When Slim found out that Stacy was dating another guy, he really *flew off the handle*.

K. Not very good

L. Disgusted with

_____ 7. That guy always says the wrong thing at the wrong time. He's really a *nitwit*.

M. Talking without understanding

N. Old car

_____ 8. John said he knew all the answers to the test, but he didn't know anything. He was just *talking through his hat*.

O. Nervous

P. Got extremely angry

Q. Rich

_____ 9. Slim never studies for exams. He just *goofs off*.

R. A fool

S. Bad loser

T. Tired

_____ 10. That new guy Yoko is dating always takes her to expensive restaurants. He must be really *well-heeled*.

U. From memory, without preparation

© 1997 by The Center for Applied Research in Education

1-46   Stone Soup: More Miscellaneous Slang *(Continued)*

_____   11. When Toshi asked Yuko out, she was really *in seventh heaven.*

_____   12. Gloria wanted the job badly. Before she went in for the interview, she *kept her fingers crossed.*

_____   13. I didn't know why I disliked the new neighbors. They just *rubbed me the wrong way.*

_____   14. Tod told us not to worry about the test. He said that it was a *breeze.*

_____   15. Juan always gets the highest grades in ESL. He's really *sharp.*

_____   16. I never get the highest grades in the class. I guess I'm *not so hot* in English.

_____   17. Even though I had most of the answers right, I still got a low grade. I think that was a *raw deal.*

_____   18. Slim kept bothering Stacy when she was trying to study. Finally, she told him to *knock it off.*

_____   19. After studying till 2:00 A.M., Tadeusz was really *beat.*

_____   20. Slim forgot his notes the day he had to give his oral report; so he talked *off the top of his head.*

More slang: A fat cat is a rich or important person.

© 1997 by The Center for Applied Research in Education

1-47   BESIDES, I WANT TO SIT BESIDE YOU: BESIDES, BESIDE

Beside
Near, next to
Example: I want to sit beside you.

Besides
In addition to
Example: Besides a parrot, we have goldfish and two cats.

Only 4 of the following 12 sentences use *beside* or *besides* correctly. Circle the letter of each sentence that is correct, then transfer the circled letters to the blanks immediately below, but not in the order given. Rearrange the letters to make a four-letter word that answers this riddle: What vehicle runs without gasoline?

— — — —

A. Slim likes sitting besides Stacy.

B. Besides Tod and Toshi, Sasha and Gregor tried out for the team.

C. Toshi stood besides his new American friends.

D. What subjects do you like beside gym?

E. I stood beside a pretty little stream.

F. Many students beside Yuko and Yoko are taking the English test.

G. Beside math, I'm taking English, history, science, and gym.

H. Tadeusz saw Rosa standing besides her cousin.

I. We have fun in Mrs. Sikand's class. Besides we learn a lot of biology.

J. The tall tree stood besides a clump of bushes.

K. Slim said to Stacy, "I want to sit beside you at the school play."

L. Stacy said to Slim, "I really like you, but there are other guys in my life beside you."

© 1997 by The Center for Applied Research in Education

1-48 SOMETIMES THEY THINK THEY'RE IN LOVE: SOMETIMES, SOMETIME

Sometime = In the indefinite future
Example: I'm going to study sometime.
Usually comes after the verb.

Sometimes = Occasionally
Example: Sometimes, Tadeusz studies with Toshi.
Usually comes at the beginning of a sentence.

Write either *sometimes* or *sometime* in the numbered blanks in the story below.

_____Sometimes_____ Ho Buom goes out with Hasook. _____ they have fun,
      (1)   (2)

and _____ they don't. You see, they're very different people.
         (3)

Hasook _____ likes to wear smart suits with good blouses and
             (4)

heels, but Ho Buom says, "I'll put on a suit _____, but not now."
                                      (5)

Hasook doesn't study just _____. She studies every night.
                       (6)

Ho Buom says, "Oh, I'll study _____." Ho Buom is a sports
                            (7)

nut, but Hasook thinks sports are boring, though _____ Ho Buom
                                      (8)

drags her to a soccer game. _____ she has fun. Usually,
                         (9)

she's bored. Ho Buom doesn't have much ambition. He says, "Maybe,

_____ or other, I'll go to college to play soccer." Hasook
      (10)

says, "I'm going to medical school, not just _____ but right
                              (11)

after I finish college." Ho Buom said to Hasook the other day,

"_____ you bore me. I want a party girl for a girlfriend."
   (12)

Hasook answered, "_____ you scare me. I want a guy who's
             (13)

going somewhere."

Do you think Ho Buom and Hasook should get married _____?
                                       (14)

_____ I do, and _____ I don't. You see, they're
   (15)   (16)

very different, even though _____ they think they're in love.
                       (17)

© 1997 by The Center for Applied Research in Education

SECTION TWO

GRAMMAR

2-1   WHAT'S ITS NAME: NOUNS

Nouns are often names of persons, places, and things. Look at the picture below and list as many nouns shown there as you can. Use the back of this sheet if you need more space for answers. The person who lists the most nouns is the winner.

_____   _____   _____
_____   _____   _____
_____   _____   _____
_____   _____   _____
_____   _____   _____
_____   _____   _____
_____   _____   _____
_____   _____   _____
_____   _____   _____
_____   _____   _____

© 1997 by The Center for Applied Research in Education

Name _____   Date _____

2-2   OF MICE AND MEN: NOUN PLURALS

Read the following rules about making nouns plural. Then study the puzzle clues and write the plural of each noun clue in the puzzle grid.

S plurals
One dog—Two dogs
One girl—Two girls

Irregular plurals
One man—Two men
One goose—Two geese
One ox—Two oxen
One mouse—Two mice
One fish—Two fish

O + ES plurals
One potato—Two potatoes

Y to I plurals
One lady—Two ladies

ES plurals
One box—Two boxes

ES after X, CH, SH, S
One church—Two churches

F to V plurals
One life—Two lives

© 1997 by The Center for Applied Research in Education

Puzzle Clues

Across		Down	
1.	Tooth	1.	Thief
3.	Mouse	2.	Woman
6.	Man	4.	Life
7.	Leaf	5.	Loss
9.	Child	6.	Mouse
11.	Fox	8.	Knife
14.	Boss	9.	City
18.	Song	10.	Nose
19.	Dish	12.	Ox
20.	Bush	13.	Tomato
21.	Boy	15.	Egg
		16.	Hen
		17.	Fish
		19.	Dog
		20.	Baby

Name_____ Date_____

2-3 MY BOSS'S WIFE: POSSESSIVE NOUNS

Read the rules. Write possessive nouns below each picture.

> *Rules*
>
> *Add apostrophe s ('s)*   *Add apostrophe only (')*
>
> | | |
> |---|---|
> | Boy's hat | Boys' hats |
> | Girl's eyes | Girls' eyes |
> | Dog's tail | Dogs' tails |
> | Boss's wife | Bosses' wives |
> | Child's toy | |
> | Children's toys | |
> | Man's hat | |
> | Men's hats | |

1.

_____ parachute

(Natasha)

4.

_____ ice cream cone

(Gorilla)

2.

_____ tooth

(Baby)

5.

_____ sweaters

(Skater)

3.

_____ teeth

(Baby)

© 1997 by The Center for Applied Research in Education

Name_____ Date_____

2-4 RUN, DICK, RUN: BASIC VERBS

Match the verbs and pictures below. Put the letter of the picture on the blank beside the verb.

__D__	1. Dance	A 	B	
_____	2. Talk			
_____	3. Scream			
_____	4. Eat			
_____	5. Study			
_____	6. Run			
_____	7. Stand			
_____	8. Skate	C 	D	

E    F

G    H

© 1997 by The Center for Applied Research in Education

Beginning ESL

2-5 HOP, SKIP, JUMP: MORE BASIC VERBS

Match the verbs and pictures below. Put the letters of the pictures in the blanks beside the verbs.

__D__	1. Open
_____	2. Smile
_____	3. Sit
_____	4. Dream
_____	5. Hop
_____	6. Jump
_____	7. Cry
_____	8. Sleep

A

B

C

D

E

F

G

H

© 1997 by The Center for Applied Research in Education

Name_____ Date_____

2-6 EVERYBODY SING: STILL MORE BASIC VERBS

Match the verbs and pictures below. Put the letters of the pictures in the blanks beside the verbs.

__F__ 1. Hit

_____ 2. Laugh

_____ 3. Yawn

_____ 4. Crash

_____ 5. Frown

_____ 6. Drill

_____ 7. Push

_____ 8. Sing

A

B

C

D

E

F

G

H

© 1997 by The Center for Applied Research in Education

2-7   SLIM IS SLIM: BASIC ADJECTIVES

Choose adjectives that describe the pictures below. Some of the adjectives can be used more than once. Use the back of this sheet for your answers.

Angry	Frightening	Muscular	Sick	Tall
Big	Happy	Pretty	Skinny	Thin
Cheerful	Husky	Same	Slim	Uncomfortable
Cute	Itchy	Scared	Smiling	Wild
Fierce	Little	Short	Strong	
Frightened				

1.

2.

3.

4.

5.

6.
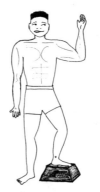

© 1997 by The Center for Applied Research in Education

© 1997 by The Center for Applied Research in Education

Name _____   Date _____

2-8   FAT CAT: ADJECTIVE-NOUN REVIEW

Write rhyming words that describe the nouns below the pictures. These words can either be adjectives or nouns used as adjectives. For example, pictured below is a *fat* cat.

1.

_____ clock

2.

_____ bird

3.

_____ box

4.

_____ bunny

5.

_____ gorilla

6.

_____ mice

7.

_____ hat

fat   cat

Beginning ESL

2-9 THICK STICK:
ADDITIONAL NOUN-ADJECTIVE REVIEW

Write rhyming words that describe the nouns below the pictures. These words can be either adjectives or nouns used as adjectives. For example, pictured here is a *thick* stick.

<u>thick</u>   <u>stick</u>

1.

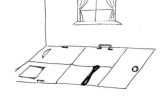

_____ door   floor

4.

_____ house

2.

_____ light

5.

_____ hat

3.

_____ fight

6.

_____ flute

© 1997 by The Center for Applied Research in Education

2-10 VERY WELL DONE: DESCRIPTIVE ADVERBS

Adverbs usually add *ly* to adjectives; however, many adverbs do not end in *ly*. Put the correct adverbs in the puzzle grids.

ly adverbs

Awfully (very)	Lovingly
Badly	Quickly
Beautifully	Rapidly
Easily	Sadly
Fairly	Skillfully
Happily	Slowly
Kindly	Softly
Loudly	Sweetly

Adverbs that do not end in ly

Fast
Hard (*Hardly = scarcely*)
Late (*Lately = recently*)
Quite
Very

A.

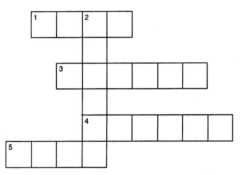

Across

1. He usually speaks _____.
3. He never speaks _____.
4. He always speaks _____.
5. Sometimes he speaks _____ loudly.

Down

2. He seldom speaks _____.

B. *Across*

2. Sometimes, he comes to school _____.
4. Sometimes, he works _____.
6. Sometimes, he comes to class _____.
7. Sometimes, he works _____ well.

Down

1. Sometimes, he works _____.
3. Sometimes he works _____ well.
5. Sometimes, he works _____ badly.

© 1997 by The Center for Applied Research in Education

2-11   Slim Sometimes Studies:
Frequency Adverbs

Write a sentence under each set of pictures. Use the correct frequency adverb.

Sample sentence: I sometimes walk to school.

100%	Always
90%	Usually
75%	Often, frequently
50%	Sometimes
10%	Rarely, seldom, infrequently
0%	Never

1.

I always walk to school._____

2.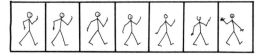

_____

3.

_____

4.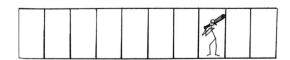

_____

5.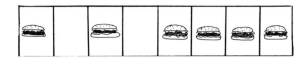

_____

6.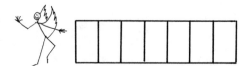

_____

© 1997 by The Center for Applied Research in Education

2-12   OUT OF THE FRYING PAN AND INTO THE FIRE: BASIC PREPOSITIONS

Put prepositions from the list below in the blanks under the pictures.

About	Behind	In front of
Above	Beside	In
At	Between	

1.

The eggs are _____in_____ the basket.

2.

The king is hiding _____ the throne.

3.

The flying saucer is _____ the trees.

4.

The teacher is standing _____ the blackboard.

5.

Stacy is standing _____ Slim and Ho Buom.

6.

Slim is thinking _____ a sports car.

7.

Slim is sitting _____ Stacy.

8.

Toshi is looking _____ Yuko.

© 1997 by The Center for Applied Research in Education

Name _____ Date _____

2-13 ON AND OFF: MORE BASIC PREPOSITIONS

Put prepositions from the list below in the blanks under the pictures.

Against	Out of	Under
Off	Over	With
On	Through	

1.

Greta is _____ water skiis.

2.

Gloria is pulling a fish _____ the water.

3.

His shoulder is _____ the wheel.

4.

Tadeusz is pushing the beans _____ the table.

5.

Greta is dancing _____ Tadeusz.

6.

The ball went _____ the window.

7.

The puppy is _____ the table.

8.

The cow jumped _____ the moon.

© 1997 by The Center for Applied Research in Education

2-14   THIS AND THAT: DEMONSTRATIVE PRONOUNS

In the grid below, shade the numbers of incorrect sentences. If your answers are correct, you will spell the most important word in the English language.

> *Demonstrative Pronouns*
>
> | *NEAR* | *FAR* |
> |---|---|
> | This is a hat. | That is a hat. |
> | I like this hat. | I like that hat. |
> | I like this. | I like that. |
> | | |
> | These are hats. | Those are hats. |
> | I like these hats. | I like those hats. |
> | I like these. | I like those. |

1. I like this.

2. I want that hats.

3. These are a hat.

4. I like those flower.

5. I want these.

6. I want those.

7. Those flowers are pretty.

8. This houses are very near.

9. This is pretty.

10. This room is big.

11. That room is small.

12. I love this guy.

13. That stars are far away.

14. These houses are in my neighborhood.

15. Those cats are noisy.

16. I want these shoes.

17. I like those candy.

18. This stores are near.

19. That gloves are blue.

20. That is an old building.

1	2	3	4	5
6	7	8	9	10
11	12	13	14	15
16	17	18	19	20

© 1997 by The Center for Applied Research in Education

2-15 YOU AND ME: PERSONAL PRONOUNS

Copy the letters of the correct answers in the empty spaces in the grid. If your answers are correct, you will spell sixteen three-letter words in the vertical spaces. You will also spell the name of a part of speech in the shaded row.

Subject pronouns	Object pronouns			
I	We	Me	Us	
You		You		*I* saw Mary.
He, she, it	They	Him, her, it	They	Mary saw *me*.

1. I like _____P_____. (P) him, (Q) he, (R) she
2. I saw _____. (D) they, (E) them, (F) her
   (two boys)
3. _____ went to a movie. (P) Us, (Q) They, (R) We
   (My friend and I)
4. John saw _____. (R) we, (S) us, (T) them
   (my friend and me)
5. _____ is my friend. (M) He, (N) Me, (O) She
   (Mary)
6. I saw _____. (N) them, (O) him, (P) they
   (two boys)
7. _____ like Slim. (A) I, (B) We, (C) They
   (one person)
8. _____ are my friends. (J) We, (K) They, (L) You
   (you and John)
9. _____ like pizza. (N) We, (O) You, (P) I
   (first-person singular)
10. _____ is pretty. (Q) He, (R) She, (S) We
    (one girl)
11. _____ can sing. (M) I, (N) He, (O) You
    (second person)
12. _____ is happy. (N) He, (O) She, (P) They
    (one boy)
13. _____ want a car. (M) Us, (N) They, (O) We
    (my friend and I)
14. _____ are kind. (T) I, (U) You, (V) He
    (two people)
15. Slim likes _____. (M) we, (N) us, (O) them
    (Tod and me)
16. Yuko likes _____. (Q) him, (R) her, (S) me
    (first person)

© 1997 by The Center for Applied Research in Education

A	P	A	U	N	O	M	A	A	A	S	A	H	N	A	A
1 P	2	3	4	5	6	7	8	9	10	11	12	13	14	15	16
E	N	E	E	T	E	N	L	E	T	N	D	T	T	T	K

Name _____ Date _____

2-16   A Boy, an Egg, and the Man in the Moon: Articles

Write the correct articles and picture names in the blanks below. The first one is done for you.

> *Rules:*
>
> *A, an* before singular nouns.
>
> *An* before words beginning with vowels: *A, E, I, O, U.*
>
> *A* before words beginning with consonants: *B, C, D, F, G, H, J, K, L, M, N, P, Q, R, S, T, V, W, X, Y, Z.*
>
> *The* before one of a kind: *the Sun*

1.

   an ape

2.

   _____

3.

   _____

4.

   _____

5.

   _____

6.

   _____

7.

   _____

8.

   _____

© 1997 by The Center for Applied Research in Education

Beginning ESL

Name_____   Date_____

2-17   A, An, The: More Articles

Write the correct articles and picture names in the blanks below. The first one is done for you.

> *Rules:*
>
> *A, an* before singular nouns.
>
> *An* before words beginning with vowels: *A, E, I, O, U.*
>
> *A* before words beginning with consonants: *B, C, D, F, G, H, J, K, L, M, N, P, Q, R, S, T, V, W, X, Y, Z.*
>
> *The* before one of a kind: *the Moon.*

1.

An umbrella
_____

4.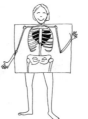

_____

7.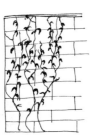

_____

2.

_____

5.

_____

8.

_____

3.

_____

6.

_____

© 1997 by The Center for Applied Research in Education

© 1997 by The Center for Applied Research in Education

Name _____ Date _____

2-18 HOW MANY WORDS ARE THERE IN GRANDMOTHER?: PARTS-OF-SPEECH REVIEW

How many words can you find in GRANDMOTHER? Arrange them in the categories below. The person who finds the most words and arranges them correctly is the winner. Nine are given to help get you started. Use another sheet of paper if you need more space for your lists.

Nouns	*Pronouns*	*Adjectives*	*Prepositions*
Age	He	Dear	At
_____	_____	_____	_____
_____	_____	_____	_____
_____	_____	_____	_____
_____	_____	_____	_____
_____	_____	_____	_____
_____	_____	_____	
_____	_____	_____	
_____	_____	_____	
_____	_____	_____	
_____	_____	_____	
_____		_____	
_____		_____	

Conjunctions	*Articles*	*Verbs*	*Negatives*
And	A	Am	No
_____	_____	_____	_____
_____	_____	_____	_____
_____	_____	_____	_____
_____		_____	
		_____	
		_____	*Names*
		_____	Ed
		_____	_____
		_____	_____
		_____	_____
		_____	_____
		_____	_____
			_____

81

2-19 I'm a Good Egg:
Subject and Verb Agreement—*Be*

Write the numbers of the correct verbs in the sentence blanks. The correct numbers in order will take you through the maze on the next page. Draw lines between the correct numbers.

A. Tadeusz __1__ a good egg. ((1) is,) (2) am, (3) are

B. Mr. and Mrs. Sikand _____ good eggs. (4) are, (5) is, (6) am

C. I _____ in America. (7) is, (8) are, (9) am

D. Our teacher _____ a good egg. (10) am, (11) are, (12) is

E. You (one person) _____ kind. (13) are, (14) is, (15) am

F. Slim and I _____ friends. (16) am, (17) is, (18) are

G. You and I _____ friends. (19) am, (20) are, (21) is

H. Toshi and you _____ good eggs. (22) am, (23) is, (24) are

I. Americans _____ good eggs. (25) am, (26) are, (27) is

J. A bee _____ an insect. (28) am, (29) are, (30) is

K. Tadeusz and Maria _____ friends. (31) am, (32) is, (33) are

L. Slim and Stacy _____ in love. (34) are, (35) is, (36) am

M. You and I and Slim _____ friends. (37) is, (38) am, (39) are

N. Yuko and Yoko _____ twins. (40) is, (41) are, (42) am

O. Bees and flies _____ insects. (43) am, (44) is, (45) are

P. Bees _____ insects. (46) is, (47) am, (48) are

Q. A horse _____ an animal. (49) am, (50) are, (51) is

R. Maria and Pedro _____ from Mexico. (52) is, (53) are

S. I _____ a student. (54) is, (55) am, (56) are

T. You and I _____ students. (57) am, (58) are, (59) is

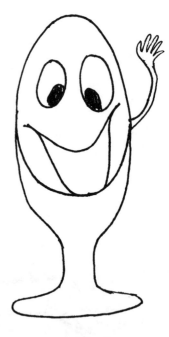

A NICE GUY

© 1997 by The Center for Applied Research in Education

2-19   I'm a Good Egg *(Continued)*

© 1997 by The Center for Applied Research in Education

Beginning ESL

Name _____ Date _____

2-20 TO BE OR NOT TO BE: NEGATIVE AGREEMENT—*BE*

Put *am not, aren't,* or *isn't* in the sentences.

> **Negative Verbs**
>
> | | | |
> |---|---|---|
> | I am not | I'm not | I am not |
> | You are not | You're not | You aren't |
> | He is not | He's not | He isn't |
> | She is not | She's not | She isn't |
> | It is not | It's not | It isn't |
> | We are not | We're not | We aren't |
> | They are not | They're not | They aren't |

1. I _____ am not _____ a police officer.
2. Mr. and Mrs. Sikand _____ dentists.
3. The book _____ red.
4. The books _____ red.
5. Slim and I _____ astronauts.
6. Tadeusz and Krystyna _____ boyfriend and girlfriend.
7. You and Mr. and Mrs. Gonzales _____ from China.
8. Monkeys _____ fish.
9. A monkey _____ a fish.
10. Rosa and Yuko _____ plumbers.
11. You and I _____ firefighters.
12. I _____ a firefighter.
13. Slim and Stacy _____ happy together.
14. Sometimes, Slim _____ a good student.
15. I _____ busy now.
16. A triangle _____ round.
17. Squares _____ round.
18. Toshi, Yoshi, and Sasha _____ photographers.
19. China _____ in North America.
20. Spring and summer _____ cold.

© 1997 by The Center for Applied Research in Education

2-21   STACY HAS A GUY:
SUBJECT AND VERB AGREEMENT—*HAVE*

Find three sentences below that have errors. The letters beside the incorrect sentences will complete this sentence:

Stacy has a guy. Slim has a ___ ___ ___.

You must rearrange the letters.

> *Subject and verb agreement: Have*
>
> | I have | We have |
> |---|---|
> | You have | You have |
> | He, she, it has | They have |

A. Stacy and Slim has each other.

B. Hasook has a boyfriend. His name is Ho Buom.

C. Yuko has a sister. Her name is Yoko.

D. George has a dictionary. It has 1,000 pages.

E. Dictionaries have thousands of words.

F. Tod and Slim have a motorcycle.

G. Tod and Slim's motorcycle have a horn.

H. Slim has a dream about a sports car.

I. Yuko and I have boyfriends.

J. Toshi and Yuko have a date.

K. You and Gregor have a date.

L. George and Gloria has good grades.

M. Sasha and Natasha have many friends.

N. Mr. and Mrs. Sikand have a baby.

O. Hans and Gretchen have a lot of homework.

© 1997 by The Center for Applied Research in Education

Name_____ Date_____

2-22   THE MONEY TREE:
SOME INDEFINITE PRONOUNS

Place the letters of the correct definitions in the sentence blanks. Then transfer the letters to the numbered blanks below these directions. If your answers are correct, you will spell the words of a popular proverb.

Patterns

Affirmative: Slim bought *something* at the store.
Slim saw *someone* he knew.
Negative: Slim didn't buy *anything*.
Slim didn't see *anyone*.
Incorrect: Slim didn't buy something. Slim didn't buy nothing.
Slim didn't see someone. Slim didn't see no one.

— — — — —   D — — — — — , —
4 6 5 2 11   1 6 2 8 5 9   3 7 6 10

— —   — — — — —.
6 5   9 7 2 2 8

1. The robber didn't take __D__. (A) anyone, (B) nothing, (C) no one, (D) anything

2. The dog was barking at _____. (E) someone, (F) anything

3. George doesn't date _____. (G) anyone, (H) anything, (I) no one

4. Natasha wanted _____ to eat. (L) anything, (M) something, (N) anyone

5. Toshi didn't see _____ he knew. (L) someone, (M) no one, (N) anyone

6. Yuko wanted _____ to drink. (O) something, (P) anyone, (Q) anything

7. Tadeusz didn't want _____ to drink. (R) anything, (S) nothing

8. Gloria waved to _____. (Q) anything, (R) anyone, (S) someone

9. The angry dog bit _____. (S) anyone, (T) someone, (U) anything

10. The police didn't arrest _____. (V) no one, (W) anyone, (X) someone

11. Maria didn't want _____ to eat. (X) something, (Y) anything, (Z) nothing

BONUS QUESTION: What is the meaning of the proverb? How would you rephrase the proverb to fit the picture on this page? How does the rephrased proverb change in meaning?

© 1997 by The Center for Applied Research in Education

2-23 SPACE SAVERS: PRONOUN CONTRACTIONS

Place the correct contractions in the blanks. The first one is done for you.

Contractions

I am . . . I'm	We are . . . We're
You are . . . You're	They are . . . They're
He is . . . He's	
She is . . . She's	
It is . . . It's	

"Who are they?"
"They're Slim's friends."

1. SLIM: _____I'm_____ a good egg.

2. STACY: Yes, _____you're_____ a good egg, but sometimes _____ lazy. You sleep all day.

3. SLIM: Maybe _____ lazy, but I love you.

4. STACY: Maybe you love me, but _____ still lazy.

5. SLIM: _____ not important. Love is important.

6. STACY: I like George. George studies all day. _____ a good student.

7. SLIM: _____ true. _____ a good student, but _____ boring. Now _____ not boring. _____ a terrific dancer.

8. STACY: _____ true. _____ a terrific dancer, but I like good students.

9. SLIM: And _____ sick of you. Maybe, I like Yuko better. She has pretty hair. _____ beautiful.

10. STACY: Both Yuko and Yoko have beautiful hair. _____ beautiful girls. So what!

11. SLIM: _____ mean.

12. STACY: _____ tired of you. Goodbye!

13. SLIM: _____ tired of me, and _____ tired of you. Listen, Stacy, _____ not boyfriend and girlfriend anymore. Maybe, _____ in love with Yuko. So goodbye!

© 1997 by The Center for Applied Research in Education

2-24 GUYS LIKE GALS:
SUBJECT AND VERB AGREEMENT—ACTION VERBS

First read the subject and verb agreement rule. Then put the letters of the correct verbs beside the sentences on the left. Next, transfer these letters to the numbered blanks below. The correct answer to number 1, for example, is *R*. Therefore, *R* is placed above *both* of the 1's in the numbered blanks. If your answers are correct, you will learn what shy Mary wrote to John in code, as she was too shy to tell him directly. Here is the coded message Mary wrote: IKE LOSES ONIONS VERY EASILY, YET OLLIE UNDERSTANDS. You will also learn the method of the code.

Basic rule: Third-person singular subjects are followed by *s* ending verbs.

Singular

First person: I like sushi.
Second person: You like sushi.
Third person: He, she, it likes sushi.

Plural

We like sushi.
You like sushi.
They like sushi.

© 1997 by The Center for Applied Research in Education

Decoded message: __ __ __ __ __   __ __ __.
      7 10 3 2 9 6 3 5

Method of code: __ __ R̲ __ __   __ __ __ __ __ R̲ __
      8 7 1 11 4 10 9 4 4 9 1 11

__R__ 1. Slim and Tod _____ a motorcycle.   R. own, S. owns

_____ 2. Boys usually _____ girls.   U. likes, V. like

_____ 3. Stacy and Slim _____ ice skating. N. enjoys, O. enjoy

_____ 4. Masha often _____ to school.   S. bike, T. bikes

_____ 5. Slim _____ a sports car.   U. want, V. wants

_____ 6. Toshi and I _____ sushi.   Y. like, Z. likes

_____ 7. Some dogs _____ too much.   H. barks, I. bark

_____ 8. The dog and cat always _____.   F. fight, G. fights

_____ 9. Mice _____ cheese.   D. eats, E. eat

_____ 10. Mr. and Mrs. Sikand _____ a new baby. K. has, L. have

_____ 11. George and Gloria often _____ together. S. study, T. studies

2-25 TO HAVE OR HAVE NOT:
NEGATIVE AGREEMENT—PRESENT ACTION VERBS

First read the negative sentence patterns. Then complete each sentence with appropriate negative verbs.

> *Patterns*
>
> I have a dog. I *don't have* a dog.
> Toshi likes pizza. Toshi *doesn't like* pizza.

1. I _____ don't _____ _____ like _____ hot peppers. I like mild peppers.

2. Juan _____ _____ hamburgers for lunch. He eats hot dogs.

3. Slim and Rosa _____ _____ to school together. Slim walks with Stacy.

4. Ho Buom _____ _____ Yuko. He loves Hasook.

5. Natasha and Boris _____ _____ Spanish. They speak Russian.

6. Gregor _____ _____ a beard. He has a mustache.

7. Turtles _____ _____ horns. They have shells.

8. Giraffes _____ _____ short necks. They have long necks.

9. A mouse _____ _____. A dog barks.

10. I _____ _____ a Swahili dictionary. I have an English dictionary.

11. Slim _____ _____ about having a motorcycle. He dreams about having a sports car.

12. Roses _____ _____ horns. They have thorns.

13. A bird _____ _____ fur. It has feathers.

14. You and I _____ _____ Portuguese. We study English.

15. Police officers _____ _____ ballet skirts. They wear uniforms.

© 1997 by The Center for Applied Research in Education

2-26   IS SLIM A BIG CHEESE?:
QUESTIONS AND SHORT ANSWERS

Following the models below, write questions and short answers for each sentence. The first one is done for you.

> Slim loves Stacy.
> *Question:* Does Slim love Stacy?
> *Short answer:* Yes, he does.
> Toshi is not happy.
> *Question:* Is Toshi happy?
> *Short answer:* No, he isn't.

1. Slim is a big cheese.   Is Slim a big cheese? Yes, he is._____

2. Yuko and Yoko are twins. _____

3. Gregor bikes to school. _____

4. George and Gloria like pizza. _____

5. You and I are students. _____

6. Toshi and Yoshi speak Japanese. _____

7. I'm from Portugal. _____

8. Some kids drive to school. _____

9. Slim has a ten-speed bike. _____

10. Slim wants a sports car. _____

11. Slim and Tod have bikes. _____

12. Maria needs a new coat. _____

13. Some girls wear too much lipstick. _____

_____

14. Slim and Tod are big cheeses. _____

_____

A big gun, a big cheese, and a big wheel are important people.

© 1997 by The Center for Applied Research in Education

Name _____   Date _____

2-27   WHERE IS SLIM?:
QUESTION WORDS WITH *TO BE*

Column A contains statements; column B, related questions; and column C, related short answers. In the blanks beside the statements in column A, put the letters from columns B and C to indicate related questions and short answers. Look at the patterns below. The first one is done for you.

Statements	*Questions*	*Short answers*
Slim is in the library.	*Where* is Slim?	In the library
Slim is in the library every afternoon.	*When* is Slim in the library?	Every afternoon
Slim is bored.	*Why* is Slim bored?	Because he is in the library

Column A

1. I am tired. <u>E</u> <u>A</u>
2. I am tired in the morning. ___ ___
3. I'm a tired student. ___ ___
4. He's in school. ___ ___
5. They are tired. ___ ___
6. He's a tired old man. ___ ___
7. They are tired at night. ___ ___
8. She's in the library. ___ ___
9. She's in the library every evening. ___ ___
10. He is sick. ___ ___

Column B

A. Who am I?
B. When are they tired?
C. Who is he?
D. When am I tired?
E. Why am I tired?
F. Where is she?
G. When is she in the library?
H. Where is he?
I. Why are they tired?
J. Why is he sick?

Column C

A. Because I go to sleep late
B. A tired old man
C. At night
D. A tired student
E. In the library
F. In school
G. In the morning
H. Because he eats too much
I. Every evening
J. Because they don't get enough sleep

Why is Boris sick?
Because he ate too much pizza.

© 1997 by The Center for Applied Research in Education

Intermediate ESL

2-28 WHEN DOES CLASS START?: QUESTION WORDS WITH ACTION VERBS

Read the sentence patterns. Then unscramble the statements, questions, or short answers.

Statement	*Question*	*Short answer*
She lives in Mexico.	Where does she live?	In Mexico
Class starts.	When does class start?	At 8:00
He is tired.	Why is he tired?	Because he works hard

1. *Statement:* His older brothers study at the University of Chicago.
   QUESTION: DO/ OLDER/ WHERE/ BROTHERS/ STUDY/ HIS

   Where do his older brothers study?

   Short answer: At the University of Chicago

2. *Statement:* Mr. and Mrs. Sikand go to India every summer.
   QUESTION: EVERY/ SIKAND/ AND/ MR./ WHERE/ MRS./ GO/ DO/ SUMMER

   _____

   Short answer: To India

   QUESTION: GO/ INDIA/ WHEN/ MR./ AND/ TO/ DO/ MRS./ SIKAND

   _____

   Short answer: Every summer

3. *Statement:* He eats a lot of candy.
   QUESTION: LOT/ WHY/ CANDY/ OF/ EAT/ DOES/ HE/ A

   _____

   Short answer: Because he likes sweets

4. *Statement:* They work at the zoo.
   QUESTION: WORK/ DO/ WHERE/ THEY

   _____

   Short answer: At the zoo

   QUESTION: Why do they work at the zoo?
   Short answer: ANIMALS/ LIKE/ THEY/ BECAUSE

   _____

5. *Statement:* UP/ O'CLOCK/ 7/ JOHN/ AT/ GETS

   _____

   QUESTION: When does John get up?
   Short answer: At 7 o'clock

© 1997 by The Center for Applied Research in Education

2-29   What Do You Think?:
Who and What as Subject and Object

The questions numbered 1 to 10 below contain two errors in the use of *what* and *who* as question words. Copy the numbers of the two errors in the blanks below these directions. If your choices are correct, you will answer the following question: IF TODAY IS THE 24TH, WHAT IS THE DATE OF THE DAY AFTER NEXT?

— —

SUN	MON	TUES	WED	THURS	FRI	SAT
24	25	26	27	28	29	30

Patterns

Who as subject: *Who* has a pencil?
What as subject: *What* has four legs and a tail?
Who(m) as object: *Who(m)* do you love?
What as object: *What* do you want for breakfast?
Note: *Do* or *does* is used when *who(m)* or *what* are objects.
          Sometimes, *whom* is used instead of *who* as object.

---

1. What do you want for breakfast?

2. What does have three wheels and a handlebar?

3. Who eats a lot of candy?

4. Who(m) do you want to marry?

5. What do Yuko and Yoko want to buy?

6. Whom always answers all the questions?

7. Who does Juan like best?

8. What sleeps all day and says "Who-Who" at night?

9. Who always gets high grades?

10. What do you mean?

Huh?

© 1997 by The Center for Applied Research in Education

2-30   QUIZ KIDS ONLY:
REVIEW OF QUESTION PATTERNS

Find the five incorrect sentences below. If your choices are correct, you will learn how NO + NO + NO = YES. You will learn this by discovering the number each letter represents. To discover this, write the numbers of the incorrect sentences in the blanks under the letters in the arithmetic problem. Do not change the order of the numbers. But remember that all the N's equal the same number, and all the O's equal the same number. The remaining three incorrect sentences will give you the number equivalents of the letters Y-E-S. Note that the numbers of the questions are *not* in numerical order.

NO   +   NO   +   NO   =   YES

4_   +   _ _   +   _ _   =   _ _ _

4. Does Yuko and Yoko have a baby sister?

5. Is Rosa cute?

6. Do Tod understand algebra?

7. Where are Gregor and Natasha going?

9. Do Yuko and Yoko always dress alike?

10. Is George going to a movie with Gloria?

11. Who does Slim go around with?

12. What do Rosa and Juan usually eat for lunch?

13. Where are Li and Siegfried going?

14. Why does Mr. Sikand speak loudly in class?

1. Does Hasook and Ho Buom plan to get married?

2. When does Slim usually get to class?

3. Is a dog and a cat good pets?

15. What time are you going home?

16. What does *curious* mean?

8. What does Gloria and George like most?

No + no + no = yes.

© 1997 by The Center for Applied Research in Education

2-31   A BOX OF CHOCOLATES AND A CARTON OF EGGS: SUBJECT AND VERB AGREEMENT—INTERVENING PHRASES

Put the letters of the correct verbs in the sentence blanks. Then transfer these letters to the numbered answer blanks below these directions. If your choices are correct, you will spell out the answer to the following problem:

A woman is driving a big car. Her headlights are off. The streetlights are not on. The moon is not shining. A small, brown rabbit runs across the street. The car quickly stops. How does the woman see the rabbit?

Number 3 is done for you. The answer is *H*. Therefore, both 3's in the numbered blanks are *H's*.

___ __H__ ___   ___ ___ ___   ___ ___   ___ __H__ ___ ___ ___ ___ ___.
 7   3   1   6   8   5   4   6   6   3   4   5   4   5   2

Rule: The verb agrees with the subject, not the nouns in an intervening phrase.

Patterns

Yes: A *box* of chocolates *is* on the table.
No: A *box* of chocolates *are* on the table.
Yes: Two *boxes* of chocolate *are* on the table.
No: Two *boxes* of chocolate *is* on the table.

---

1. The list of books _____ on the desk.   (E) is, (F) are
2. The boxes of candy _____ first.   (G) sell, (H) sells
3. The bag of potatoes ___H___ ten pounds.   (G) weigh, (H) weighs
4. The students in my ESL class _____ hard.   (I) work, (J) works
5. A can of garbage _____ flies.   (M) bring, (N) brings
6. The noises of highway construction   (S) hurt, (T) hurts
    _____ my ears.
7. A person with two cars probably _____   (T) spends, (U) spend
    a lot for gas.
8. A student on two athletic teams _____   (U) practices, (V) practice
    long hours.

A box of chocolates *is* a great gift.

© 1997 by The Center for Applied Research in Education

2-32   WILL YOU, WON'T YOU?: FUTURE TENSE—*WILL*

Fill in the blanks in the story with contracted forms of *will* or with *will* or *won't*.

> **Patterns**
> I, you, he, she, it, we, they will
> *Negative:* I, you, he, she, it, we, they won't (will not)
>
> *Contracted forms of will:*
>
> I will . . . I'll   We will . . . We'll
> You will . . . You'll
> He will . . . He'll   They will . . . They'll
> She will . . . She'll
> It will . . . It'll

1. Ho Buom said to Hasook, "_____Will_____ you marry me?" Hasook answered, "No,

2. I _____won't_____. _____I'll_____ never marry you." Ho Buom said,
   (negative)   (contraction)

3. "I think _____ marry me when you see how much _____
            (contraction)   (contraction)

4. make playing professional football." Hasook said, "I think _____
                                                              (contraction)

5. marry George. _____ make more money as a doctor than you ever
                 (contraction)

6. _____. Anyway, if I marry you, _____ fight all the time.
                                              (contraction)

7. The only thing you like is football, and _____ never change. We
                                            (contraction)

8. _____ be happy unless you change, and I know you _____.
   (negative)   (negative)

9. Now Yuko and Toshi _____ be happy together because they have the

10. same mind. _____ always have the same values. That's why
               (contraction)

11. _____ be happy." Ho Buom laughed and whispered, "I know
    (contraction)

12. _____ marry me because you love me. For the last time, _____
    (contraction)

13. you marry me?" "No, I _____," said Hasook. Then he kissed
                          (negative)

14. her, and she said, "Well, maybe, I _____ , and maybe I _____."
                                                                       (negative)

© 1997 by The Center for Applied Research in Education

2-33   I'M GOING TO BE YOUR GIRLFRIEND: FUTURE TENSE—*BE GOING*

Sometimes, forms of *be going* express future time. Read the patterns. Then fill in the blanks in the story with correct forms of *be going*.

Statements

I am going to a party. I am going to have fun.
You (We) (They) are going.
He (She) (It) is going.

Questions

Am I going?
Are you (we) (they) going?
Is he (she) (it) going?

Short answers

Yes, I am. No, I'm not.
Yes, you (we) (they) are. No, we're not.
Yes, he (she) (it) is. No, it's not.

Boris is new in America. He is thinking, "This (1) _____is going to be_____ rough

(hard). It (2) _____ a long time before I speak English well. My

brothers and I (3) _____not_____ make friends for ages (for a long

time). I (4) _____ feel lonely and homesick." Boris is scared the

first day of school. But the ESL teacher is Mr. Sikand from India. He understands what it's

like to be a stranger in a new land. Mr. Sikand says, "First, we

(5) _____ introduce ourselves." Boris meets lots of students from

many countries. Best of all, he meets Natasha. After class, Natasha asks Boris,

(6) _____you_____ in the cafeteria?" Boris answers, "Yes, I

(7) _____ in the cafeteria. Will you eat lunch with me?" Natasha

says, "Yes. In fact, I (8) _____ lunch with you every day. Some-

times, I get tired of speaking English. We can speak Russian together." Boris asks, "Natasha,

(9) _____you_____ my girlfriend?" Natasha says, "Yes, I

(10) _____." Then she says, "Do you think we

(11) _____ have fun in America?" Boris answers, "Yes, I think we

(12) _____. But first of all, (13) _____you_____

the school dance with me?" Natasha answers, "Yes, I (14) _____."

Boris isn't frightened or lonely anymore. He thinks, "I

(15) _____not_____ unhappy in America after all."

© 1997 by The Center for Applied Research in Education

2-34 WHAT'S HE DOING?: PRESENT PROGRESSIVE, YES/NO, AND INFORMATION QUESTIONS AND ANSWERS

Study the patterns. Then select the answers for each of the questions below. Next, circle your answer letters in the grid. If your choices are correct, you will complete the following rules: THE PRESENT PROGRESSIVE EXPRESSES ACTION HAPPENING _____. THE PRESENT PROGRESSIVE ENDS IN _____.

Yes/no question
Is Slim studying?

Information questions

What is Slim doing?
Where is Slim studying?
When is Slim leaving?
Why is Slim studying?

Short answer
Yes, he is. No he isn't.

Short answers

Studying.
In the library.
At 10 o'clock.
Because he has a test.

© 1997 by The Center for Applied Research in Education

1. Is Slim making eyes at Stacy?
   - (L) Because he likes her.
   - (M) After school.
   - (N) Yes, he is.

2. What is Slim doing?

   - (O) Studying for a test.
   - (P) In the library.
   - (Q) At 5:00.

3. Why is George raising his hand?

   - (W) Because he knows the answer.
   - (X) In class.
   - (Y) On Friday.

4. Where is Krystyna now?

   - (H) Skiing.
   - (I) In Colorado.
   - (J) Yesterday morning.

5. When is Toshi going to Yuko's house?

   - (E) Because he likes her.
   - (F) Studying.
   - (G) At 7 o'clock.

L	I	N	G	Y
P	E	O	J	Q
X	R	W	F	M

2-35   STRANGER THAN FICTION: NEGATIVE FORMS OF PRESENT AND PRESENT PROGRESSIVE

Following the patterns in the model sentences below, write three sentences under each picture.

Model sentences

What is the kangaroo doing?

1. *Present progressive:*
   The kangaroo is carrying a human baby in its pouch.

2. *Present progressive, negative:*
   The kangaroo isn't carrying a baby kangaroo in its pouch in this picture.

3. *Present tense:*
   Kangaroos carry baby kangaroos in their pouches.

4. *Present, negative:*
   Kangaroos don't carry human babies in their pouches.

What is the dog doing?

1. <u>The dog is climbing a tree.</u>

2. <u>A cat isn't climbing a tree in this picture.</u>

3. <u>Cats climb trees.</u>

4. <u>Dogs don't climb trees.</u>

What is the automobile doing?

1. _____
   _____

2. The automobile _____
   traveling on the ground in this picture.

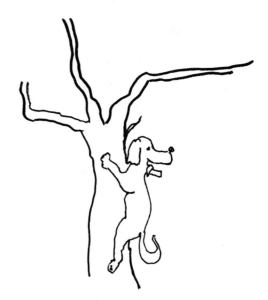

© 1997 by The Center for Applied Research in Education

3. Airplanes _____

4. Automobiles _____

What is the cat doing?

1. _____

   _____

2. A man _____

   _____

3. Men _____

4. Cats _____

What is the octopus eating?

1. _____

   _____

2. A person _____

   _____

3. People _____

4. Octopuses _____

   _____

© 1997 by The Center for Applied Research in Education

2-36   I LOVE YOU:
PROGRESSIVE AND NON-PROGRESSIVE VERBS

Some verbs aren't used in the progressive even for *now* situations. For example, we don't say, "I am seeing a bird." We say, "I see a bird." We don't say, "I am hearing thunder." We say, "I hear thunder." If the progressive (or *ing*) verb sounds right to you in the sentences below, find a place for it in the grid. You must use the present form of each verb. One is done for you.

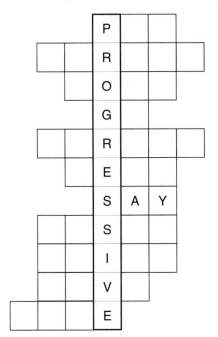

1.   The little girl is *saying* the alphabet.

2.   Ho Buom said to Hasook, "I am *loving* you."

3.   I'm *going* home now.

4.   Natasha is *feeding* the birds.

5.   The police are *arresting* two men.

6.   Slim isn't *owning* a Jaguar.

7.   I am *fearing* mice.

8.   Slim is *wanting* a sportscar.

9.   Ho Buom lifted weights this morning. Now, he is *resting*.

10.   Mr. and Mrs. Sikand are *arriving* in New York at 10:00 P.M.

11.   Pedro is *bringing* Maria candy and flowers.

12.   I am not *believing* in ghosts.

13.   Hasook is *hoping* to go to college in the fall.

14.   Juan is *needing* a new notebook.

15.   "Hi, Li, I am *knowing* you from ESL class."

16.   Slim is *saving* money for a new car.

17.   Masha is *remembering* her grandmother well.

18.   Mrs. Sikand is *paying* her monthly bills.

19.   Mrs. Sikand is *giving* a test this Friday.

20.   Yuko is *preferring* a white dress for the prom.

© 1997 by The Center for Applied Research in Education

2-37 EITHER/OR: VERBS THAT ARE BOTH PROGRESSIVE AND NON-PROGRESSIVE

Some verbs can be used in both the progressive and non-progressive forms with different meanings. Study the verbs below and circle the letters of *correct* sentences. Then place these letters in order in the blanks immediately above the sentences. If your choices are correct, you will learn why Mary likes *theater* and not *opera, them* and not *us, ants* and not *bees.*

Non-progressive	*Progressive*
Opinion: I think Mr. Sikand is a good teacher.	*Thoughts about:* I am thinking about my girlfriend.
Ownership: I have a bike.	*Idiomatic uses:*
	I am having a good time.
	I am having fun.
	I am having a party.
	I am having dinner. (eating)
	Mrs. Sikand is having a baby. (giving birth)

Mary likes words that begin with __A__ __ __ __ __ __ __ __.

A. My sister is having a big wedding.
B. Mrs. Sikand is have a dog.
D. Slim is having a dictionary.
F. Stacy is have a new red dress.
R. Slim is thinking about Stacy.
M. I am think that George is a good student.
N. I am have a party tonight.
T. Rosa has a dog.
I. Stacy is having fun with Yuko and Yoko.
X. The school is have a big gym.
Y. I am have pizza for dinner tonight.
C. I think that the principal is a kind man.
P. I am think that algebra is hard.
Q. I am have fun now.
U. I am have a party tonight.
L. I am thinking about my grandparents in Seoul.
G. I am have sushi for dinner.
H. Mrs. Sikand is have a baby.
E. George thinks Kennedy was a great president.
S. We are having bacon and eggs for breakfast.

© 1997 by The Center for Applied Research in Education

Name _____ Date _____

2-38 THE ROAST IS SMELLING GOOD: MORE VERBS THAT ARE BOTH PROGRESSIVE AND NON-PROGRESSIVE

Some verbs can be used in both progressive and non-progressive forms, but with different meanings. Study the verbs below. Then circle the letters beside the *incorrect* sentences. The number of errors will provide the answer to the following arithmetic problem:

$$16 \times 4 \times 18 - 12 \times 9 \times 0 = \underline{\hspace{2cm}}.$$

Verb Patterns

Progressive: Used with action verbs.

Non-progressive: Used with non-action. The word that follows the verb refers to the subject.

1. She is *tasting* the new food.   The food *tastes* good.
2. The dog is *smelling* the meat.   The meat *smells* good.
3. The butcher is *weighing* the meat.   The meat *weighs* one pound.
4. She is *looking* at the sky.   She *looks* beautiful.

A. She *looks* 16.

B. Yoko is *looking* at her sister.

C. My mother is *tasting* the soup.

D. The soup *tastes* funny.

E. The package *looks* heavy.

F. The dog is *smelling* the man's hand.

G. The garbage *smells* terrible.

H. The doctor is *weighing* the baby.

I. The baby *weighs* 7 pounds.

J. She *looks* unhappy.

The roast is
smelling a rose.
(*Smell* as action verb.)

© 1997 by The Center for Applied Research in Education

2-39   NO NUMBERS IN THIS ONE: IRREGULAR VERBS

Irregular verbs generally do not use *ed* to form the past and past participle. Place the verbs below, which are grouped by number of letters, in the puzzle grid. To help you, letters of some verbs appear in the grid. *Hint:* Study the puzzle grid first, find the number of letters in the word, and then look at the clues.

Two-Letter Verbs

Across

do

Down

go

Four-Letter Verbs

Across

beat	lead
come	lend
deal	make
feed	ring
find	sing
hurt	spin
keep	tear
know	wear

Down

bend	lose
blow	meet
burn	read
draw	ride
fall	rise
give	sink
hear	tell
hold	weep

Three-Letter Verbs

Across

eat	run
put	see
rid	

Down

cut	get
dig	say

Five-Letter Verbs

Across

arise	slide
begin	steal
bleed	swing
break	teach
drink	throw
leave	

Down

awake	sting
drive	think
flight	write
kneel	
speak	

Six-Letter Verbs

Across

choose

Down

become

© 1997 by The Center for Applied Research in Education

2-40   HIDE AND SEEK: MORE IRREGULAR VERBS

Within each of the words in the word list below is a hidden irregular verb. Circle the verb; then write the past and past participle of each verb in the blanks beside it. The first one is done for you.

1. (Bear)d   bore   born, borne

2. Doom   _____   _____

3. Meat   _____   _____

4. Splendid   _____   _____

5. Goat   _____   _____

6. Pliers   _____   _____

7. Players   _____   _____

8. Plight   _____   _____

9. Close   _____   _____

10. Bedspread   _____   _____

11. Strident   _____   _____

12. String   _____   _____

13. Surprise   _____   _____

14. Grown-up   _____   _____

15. Settle   _____   _____

16. Stake   _____   _____

17. Sweepstakes   _____   _____

18. Window   _____   _____

19. Shower   _____   _____

20. Plead   _____   _____

21. Sputter   _____   _____

22. Riddle   _____   _____

23. Stealth   _____   _____

24. Letter   _____   _____

25. Better   _____   _____

26. Digit   _____   _____

27. Drawer   _____   _____

28. Breakfast   _____   _____

© 1997 by The Center for Applied Research in Education

2-41 ADD-ONS:
MORE PRACTICE WITH IRREGULAR VERBS

This activity will help you remember irregular verbs—verbs that do not add *ed* to form the past and past participle. Add one letter to each of the words below to form a common irregular verb. Then write the past and past participle of each verb you form. The first one is done for you. (One letter is missing in each!)

1. tea_r_   _____tore_____   _____torn_____
2. fin___   _____   _____
3. ___at   _____   _____
4. wee___   _____   _____
5. sin___   _____   _____
6. shin___   _____   _____
7. ___row   _____   _____
8. ___ring   _____   _____
         _____
9. ___rind   _____   _____
10. ___pit   _____   _____
11. ___raw   _____   _____
12. ___low   _____   _____
13. knee___   _____   _____
14. ___it   _____   _____
         _____
15. hi___   _____   _____
16. forge___   _____   _____
17. ___end   _____   _____
18. ___ear   _____   _____
19. ___each   _____   _____
20. bin___   _____   _____
21. ben___   _____   _____
22. ___all   _____   _____

© 1997 by The Center for Applied Research in Education

© 1997 by The Center for Applied Research in Education

Name _____   Date _____

2-42   DID YOU EVER SEE A LAUGHING HYENA?:
PAST TENSE—*EVER* AND *NEVER*

Study the patterns. Then write a negative answer to each question.

Were you ever at the zoo? *No, I was never at the zoo.*		Did you ever see a laughing hyena? *No, I never saw a laughing hyena.*

1. Did you ever buy fancy
   duds? (*fancy clothes*)

    _____

   _____

2. Were you ever in the doghouse?
   (*in trouble*)

    _____

   _____

3. Did you ever go on a blind date?
   (*a date with someone you don't
   know*)

    _____

   _____

4. Were you ever in hot water?
   (*in trouble*)

    _____

   _____

5. Did you ever have butterflies
   in your stomach? (*become nervous*)

    _____

   _____

6. Did you ever play with fire?
   (*do something dangerous*)

    _____

   _____

7. Did you ever meet a bad egg?
   (*a bad person*)

    _____

   _____

Intermediate ESL

2-43   WERE YOU OUT WITH A CUTE CHICK LAST NIGHT?: PAST TENSE QUESTIONS AND ANSWERS

Following the patterns below, answer the questions under all the pictures.

<table>
<tr><td colspan="3">Patterns</td></tr>
<tr><td>Did you see a laughing hyena at the zoo?
I saw a laughing hyena at the zoo.
I didn't see a laughing hyena at the zoo.</td><td>OR</td><td>Were you at the zoo last week?
I was at the zoo last week.
I wasn't at the zoo last week.</td></tr>
</table>

1. Cute chick = pretty girl

    Were you out with a cute chick last night?

    Yes, _____.

    No, _____.

2. Let down your hair = relax

    Did Rosa let down her hair at Gregor's birthday party?

    Yes, _____.

    No, _____.

3. Chicken feed = small amount of money

    Did Slim sell his car for chicken feed?

    Yes, _____.

    No, _____.

© 1997 by The Center for Applied Research in Education

2-43 WERE YOU OUT WITH A CUTE CHICK LAST NIGHT? *(CONTINUED)*

4. Lose head = like someone so much you can't think clearly

   Did Gregor lose his head over Natasha?

   Yes, _____.

   No, _____.

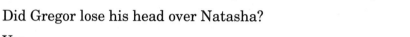

5. Hit the books = study

   Did George hit the books before the history test?

   Yes, _____.

   No, _____.

6. Spread self too thin = do too many things

   You have a part-time job. Did you spread yourself too thin during exam week?

   Yes, _____.

   No, _____.

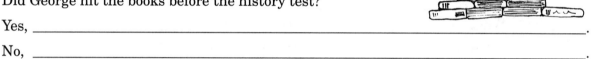

7. Sour puss = a person who doesn't laugh or smile (puss = cat)

   Was I out with a sour puss last night?

   Yes, _____.

   No, _____.

© 1997 by The Center for Applied Research in Education

2-44   DID YOU, DIDN'T YOU?:
MORE PAST TENSE QUESTIONS AND ANSWERS

Study the patterns and put the correct verbs in the blanks.

> *Patterns*
>
> Did Slim call Stacy?   Was Slim honest?
> Yes, he did. No, he didn't.   Yes, he was. No, he wasn't.

1. STACY: Slim (do) _____did_____ you (call) _____call_____ me last night?
2. SLIM: I (do not) _____.
3. STACY: But you (promise) _____ to call me.
4. SLIM: I know I (promise) _____ to call you. I (be) _____ busy.
5. STACY: Why (be) _____ you busy?
6. SLIM: I (have) _____ to study.
7. STACY: What (do) _____ you (have) _____ to study?
8. SLIM: I (have) _____ to study American history.
9. STACY: What (do) _____ you (study) _____ in American history?
10. SLIM: I (read) _____ about the Revolutionary War.
11. STACY: What (do) _____ you (read) _____ about it?
12. SLIM: I (read) _____ about America and England.
13. STACY: What (do) _____ you (learn) _____?
14. SLIM: I (learn) _____ America and England (fight) _____ France.
15. STACY: What?!!? America and England (not fight) _____ against France. America (make) _____ war against England. You (not study) _____ last night. What (do) _____ you (do) _____? I think you (go) _____ out with Yuko.
16. SLIM: I (not go) _____ out with Yuko. I (go) _____ with Yoko.
17. STACY: I hate you. You (break) _____ your promise.
18. SLIM: Yes, I (break) _____ my promise. I hope I (not break) _____ your heart.
19. STACY: No, you (do not) _____, but you've just (break) _____ off our relationship. Goodbye forever!

© 1997 by The Center for Applied Research in Education

© 1997 by The Center for Applied Research in Education

Name_____   Date_____

2-45   I Saw a Laughing Hyena in My Yard Yesterday: Past and Present Perfect

Study the patterns below and put the letters of the correct verbs in the sentence blanks. Then transfer the letters to the correct spaces in the numbered grid. If your choices are correct, you will spell four words that read the same both up and down and across.

Patterns

Past tense: Used for specified time.
I ate dinner at 6:00.

Present perfect: *Have* or *has* plus past participle.
                 Used for unspecified time.
I have never eaten at Burger King.
I haven't bought my books yet.

1 I	2	3	4
5	6	7	8
9	10	11	12
13	14	15	16

1. I _____I_____ at Burger King yesterday.
   (I) ate, (J) have eaten

2. I _____ at Burger King many times.
   (C) ate, (D) have eaten

3. _____ at Burger King yet?
   (D) Ate, (E) Have you eaten

4. _____ that movie twice or three times?
   (B) See, (A) Have you seen

2-45   I Saw a Laughing Hyena in My Yard Yesterday (Continued)

5. _____ the school play yet?
       (C) See, (D) Have you seen

6. I've never _____ on the roller coaster.
              (D) rode, (E) ridden

7. I _____ on the roller coaster last night.
       (A) rode, (B) have ridden

8. I _____ to New York over Christmas vacation.
       (M) have gone, (N) went

9. I _____ a laughing hyena.
       (E) have never seen, (F) seen

10. I _____ a laughing hyena at the zoo yesterday.
        (A) didn't see, (B) have never seen

11. I _____ with a famous movie star last night.
        (R) have danced, (S) danced

12. I _____ with famous movie stars four times.
        (S) danced, (T) have danced

13. I _____ an *A* on the test last Friday.
        (A) got, (B) have gotten

14. I _____ lots of *A*'s.
        (M) got, (N) have gotten

15. I _____ to New York in February.
        (T) flew, (U) have flown

16. I _____ to New York five or six times.
        (S) have flown, (T) flew

© 1997 by The Center for Applied Research in Education

2-46   I Haven't Seen You for Ages: Present Perfect—*For* or *Since*

Study the patterns. Then count the incorrect sentences. If you are correct, the total number of incorrect sentences will provide the answer for the arithmetic problem below. Follow the directions carefully!

Directions

A.   Write a number—any number—on a piece of paper.
B.   Add 9 to that number.
C.   Double the new number.
D.   Subtract 4 from your doubled number.
E.   Divide this number by 2.
F.   Subtract the first number you chose.

Patterns

Present perfect plus "for" phrase: length of time.
   I have been in America for ten months.

Present perfect plus "since" phrase or clause: a specific time.
   I have lived in Boston since 1994.

Sentences

1.   Slim has dated Stacy since two years.
2.   I have wanted to learn English since I was a child.
3.   My mother has wanted to come to America since all her life.
4.   I have enjoyed Japanese food for I met Yuko.
5.   I have enjoyed Japanese food for ages.
6.   I have loved Mexican food since ages.
7.   Mr. and Mrs. Sikand have been married since 1992.
8.   Boris has liked Natasha since five months.
9.   I have belonged to the foreign students' club for February.
10. Stacy and Slim haven't fought for five days.
11. The doorbell has rung since ten minutes.
12. I have been in the library since 9:00 this morning.
13. Nisme sang for one half hour.
14. Toshi has known Yoko since he came to America.
15. Tod hasn't bought any new clothes for a year.

© 1997 by The Center for Applied Research in Education

2-47   SLIM HAD SPENT ALL HIS MONEY: PAST PERFECT

The past perfect is formed with *had* plus the past participle. It expresses action completed before a definite time in the past. Study the model and complete the past perfect sentences under each picture.

Model:

Stacy's birthday was on Wednesday. Slim spent all his money on Tuesday. By the time Stacy's birthday came, <u>Slim had spent all his money</u>.

1.

The cat sat on the hat in the morning. I came in the afternoon.
By the time I came, _____

_____.

2.

The prisoner escaped at 5:00 A.M. The guard came at 5:30 A.M.
By the time the guard came, _____

_____.

3.

It began to rain at 11:00. Juan left his house at 11:15.
When Juan _____,

it had already _____.

© 1997 by The Center for Applied Research in Education

2-47   SLIM HAD SPEND ALL HIS MONEY
(CONTINUED)

4.

The bee stung the baby at 10:00. Mother came running at 10:05.

When mother _____,

the bee _____.

5.

Gregor's mom got to the game late. Gregor made a basket early in the game.

By the time Gregor's mom _____

_____

6.

In the morning the escaped gorilla broke into a bakery and ate fifteen pies. The police captured the gorilla two hours later.

By the time the police captured the gorilla, he _____

_____.

© 1997 by The Center for Applied Research in Education

2-48   WHERE WAS MARTIN WHEN THE LIGHTS WENT OUT?: PAST PROGRESSIVE

Past progressive refers to action that was in progress at a definite time in the past. Study the patterns below and write past progressive sentences under each picture. The first one is partially done for you.

> *Patterns:*
>
> What were you doing when the telephone rang?
> I was studying when the telephone rang.
> OR
> When the telephone rang, I was studying.

1.

What was the monkey doing when he fell out of the tree?

_____.

OR

When _____.

2.

What was Martin doing when the lights went out?

Martin was standing in the dark _____.

OR

When _____.

3.

What was Big Hunk doing when he sprained his ankle?

© 1997 by The Center for Applied Research in Education

2-48　Where Was Martin When the Lights Went Out? (Continued)

Big Hunk was playing ice hockey _____.

OR

When _____.

4.

What was Olaf doing when he got tangled up in a tree?

Olaf _____.

OR

When _____.

5.

What was Masha doing when she hit her finger with a hammer?

Masha was building a bookcase _____.

OR

When _____.

6.

What was Nerd doing when he broke his tooth?

Nerd was putting his foot in his mouth _____.

OR

When _____.

© 1997 by The Center for Applied Research in Education

2-49 WHAT'LL YOU BE DOING TONIGHT?: FUTURE PROGRESSIVE

The future progressive refers to action that will be in progress in the future. The future progressive emphasizes that the action will occur over an extended period of time. Read the patterns below and answer each question in your own words, using the two forms of the future progressive.

> **Patterns**
>
> The future progressive is formed with *will be* plus the present participle (*ing* verb) **or** with a form of *be going* plus the present participle.
>
> 1. I will be studying tonight.
> 2. I am going to be studying tonight.

A. What will you be doing tonight?

1._____

2._____

B. What will you be doing this afternoon?

1._____

2._____

C. What will you be doing this weekend?

1._____

2._____

D. What will you be doing next summer?

1._____

2._____

E. What will you be doing after you are graduated from high school?

1._____

2._____

© 1997 by The Center for Applied Research in Education

2-50 HE'D BEEN WORKING ALL DAY: PRESENT AND PAST PERFECT PROGRESSIVE

Select the correct verb for each sentence blank. Circle the letter beside that verb. Then transfer the circled letters to the numbered blanks below these directions. If your answers are correct, you will spell a five-word palindrome—a group of words that reads the same backwards and forward. The first one is done for you.

$$\frac{A}{1} \quad \frac{A}{4} \frac{}{1} \frac{}{5} \cdot \frac{A}{1} \quad \frac{}{4} \frac{}{3} \frac{A}{1} \frac{}{5} \quad \frac{A}{1} \quad \frac{}{2} \frac{A}{1} \frac{}{5} \frac{}{1} \frac{A}{3}$$

$$\frac{}{6} \frac{A}{1} \frac{}{5} \frac{A}{1} \frac{}{4} \frac{A}{1}$$

Present perfect progressive

I have been working.   Expresses action of extended duration
He has been working.   that began in the past and continues
                              in the present.
    I have been living in New York for two years.
    I have been living in New York since 1955.

Past perfect progressive

I had been working.   Expresses action of extended duration
He had been working.   that was completed before a definite
                              time in the past.
    By March 1995, I had been living in New York for three years.

---

1. The kids started working at 2:00 P.M. It is now 5:00 P.M. The kids are tired because they _____ for three hours. (A) have been working, (B) had been working

2. Ho Buom began lifting weights at 6:00 P.M. When the gym closed at 10:00 P.M., he _____ for four hours. (C) had been lifting weights, (D) has been lifting weights, (E) was lifting weights

3. Boris is going away, and Masha is crying. Her eyes are red because she _____ for nearly two hours. (I) is crying, (J) was crying, (K) had been crying, (L) has been crying

4. Masha's eyes were red. She _____ all day because Boris was going away. (M) had been sobbing, (N) has been sobbing

5. Gregor had the flu. He went to the doctor's office at 1:00 P.M. The doctor was very busy. When the doctor finally saw him, he _____ for an hour and a half. (N) had been waiting, (O) has been waiting

6. George has an exam Monday morning. He began studying at 8:00 A.M. Sunday morning. By 8:00 P.M., he _____ for twelve hours. (P) had been studying, (Q) has been studying, (R) is studying, (S) was studying

© 1997 by The Center for Applied Research in Education

2-51 THREE UGLY MONSTERS: COMPARISON OF ADJECTIVES—ONE SYLLABLE, THREE SYLLABLES, Y ENDINGS

Read the rules. Then complete the sentences next to each picture, using the words in parentheses. The first one is done for you.

Rules

1. One-syllable adjectives are compared by adding *er* or *est*.
   An elephant is *bigger* than a horse.
   An elephant is the *biggest* of all animals.

2. When adjectives end in *y*, change the *y* to *i* and add *er* or *est*.
   Marcy is *friendlier* than Catrina.
   Marcy is the *friendliest* girl in the class.

3. Adjectives of three or more syllables are compared with *more* or *most*.
   A car is *more expensive* than a bicycle.
   A Rolls Royce is the *most expensive* of all cars.

A.

1. The first package (small) <u>is smaller than</u> the third package.

2. The first package (small) _____ _____ the second package.

3. The third package (large) _____ _____ the first package.

4. The third package (beautiful) _____ _____ first package.

5. The third package (beautiful) _____ _____ the second package.

6. The second package (beautiful) _____ _____ the first package.

7. The third package (beautiful) _____ _____ of the three.

© 1997 by The Center for Applied Research in Education

2-51   THREE UGLY MONSTERS *(CONTINUED)*

B. Look at the pictures of Bo, Mo, and Zo. Then complete the sentences telling what you think about the three monsters. Two are done for you.

1. Bo is (ugly) <u>uglier</u> than <u>Zo.</u>

2. Mo is (fierce) _____ than _____ .

3. Zo is (dangerous) _____ than _____ .

4. Bo isn't (wild) _____ than _____ .

5. Bo isn't (horrible) _____ than _____ .

6. Mo isn't (frightening) _____ than _____ .

7. Zo isn't (ferocious) _____ than _____ .

8. Mo is (silly) _____ than _____ .

9. (ugly) <u>Zo is</u> the <u>ugliest</u> of the three.

10. (silly) _____ the _____ of the three.

11. (mean) _____ the _____ of the three.

12. (dangerous) _____ the _____ of the three.

13. (frightening) _____ the _____ of the three.

14. (fierce) _____ the _____ of the three.

Zo

Bo

Mo

© 1997 by The Center for Applied Research in Education

Intermediate ESL

2-52   THE "WORSTEST" PIE: IRREGULARLY COMPARED ADJECTIVES, DOUBLE COMPARATIVES, AND SUPERLATIVES

Circle the numbers of the incorrect sentences. Then transfer the numbers of both correct and incorrect sentences to the score chart. The totals of both columns will provide the answer to the following problem: A rope is 1,027 feet long. If you cut it into 1,027 pieces, how many times will you cut through the rope?

Irregularly compared adjectives:

Good, better, best	well, better, best	little, less, least
bad, worse, worst	many, more, most	much, more, most
far, farther, farthest or further, furthest		

Double comparatives and superlatives:

Correct: He has a worse cold than I do.
Incorrect: He has a worser cold than I do.
Correct: This is the worst pie I have ever eaten.
Incorrect: This is the worstest pie I have ever eaten.

© 1997 by The Center for Applied Research in Education

	Correct	Incorrect
		2
Totals:		

1.   After the performance, Maria got the most applause.

2.   Slim said, "This is the worstest pie I've ever eaten."

3.   Is Yoko more beautiful than Yuko?

4.   She is the bestest writer in the class.

5.   He is more taller than his brother.

6.   He has less money than his brother.

7.   The president is more powerfuller than the vice-president.

8.   That criminal is the baddest man in the United States.

Name_____   Date_____

2-53   AS EASY AS PIE: COMPARISONS WITH *As*

Write sentences under each pair of pictures. Follow one or more of the patterns illustrated.

Patterns

lemon pie   **pecan pie**   **apple pie**   **pumpkin pie**

A. The lemon pie is as big as the pecan pie.
B. The lemon pie isn't as big as the apple pie.
C. The apple pie is nearly as big as the pumpkin pie.

1.

Gloria   **Mr. Jones**

(*hungry*) Gloria _____ Mr. Jones.

(*young*) Mr. Jones _____ Gloria.

(*old*) Gloria _____ Mr. Jones.

2.

Nerd   **Nerda**

(*long*) Nerd's nose _____ Nerda's.

(*short*) Nerda's nose _____ Nerd's.

(*long*) Nerd's nose _____ nearly _____ Nerda's.

3.

Olaf   **George**

(*alert*) Olaf _____ George.

(*sleepy*) George _____ Olaf.

Intermediate ESL

© 1997 by The Center for Applied Research in Education

2-54 A SITTING DUCK:
PRESENT PARTICIPLES AS ADJECTIVES

Sometimes present participles or the *ing* form of verbs are used as adjectives. From the list below, choose the correct present participle for each picture.

List of present participles

Bowling	Frightening	Sitting
Diving	Laughing	Speeding
Flying	Weeping	

1.

_____ ball

2.

_____ board

3.

_____ beast
(animal)

4.

_____ car

5.

_____ willow
(a tree with bending branches that seems to be crying)

6.

_____ saucer

7.

_____ duck
(an easy target)

8.

_____ hyena

© 1997 by The Center for Applied Research in Education

2-55   THE TWO-HEADED MAN: NOUN PLUS *ED* AS ADJECTIVE

Sometimes nouns plus *ed* are used as adjectives, as in bald-*headed* man or sharp-*clawed* cat. Sometimes an adjective precedes the *ed*-ending noun. Write the appropriate *ed* noun-adjective and noun under each picture. The first one is done for you.

1.

__Two-headed man_____

5.

_____ man

2.

_____ woman

6.

Long _____ woman

3.

Open _____ bird

7.

Long _____ girl

4.

_____ man

8.

Double _____ man

© 1997 by The Center for Applied Research in Education

2-56   A WORRIED MOM:
MORE NOUN-PLUS-*ED* ADJECTIVES

Sometimes nouns plus *ed* are used as adjectives, as in *worried mom*. Sometimes an adjective comes before the *ed* ending noun, as in *sad-eyed dog*. Write appropriate *ed* noun-adjectives and nouns under the pictures below.

1.

Long _____ necked woman _____

5.

_____

2.

Long _____

6.

_____

3.

One _____

7.

_____

4.

Long _____

8.

_____

© 1997 by The Center for Applied Research in Education

Name _____   Date _____

2-57   A BROKEN HEART:
PAST PARTICIPLES AS ADJECTIVES

Select past participles for each of the sentence blanks. Place the letter of each past participle in the blank beside the sentence letter. These paired letters will enable you to decode the cryptogram below. The answer to sentence *A* is *E* (Known). Therefore, the *A*'s in the cryptogram equal *E*. If your choices are correct, you will spell the title of a famous collection of short stories. This title contains a past participle used as an adjective.

```
__  __  __  E  __        __  __  __  __        __  __  __  E  __
 B   D   C   E  A         B   F   G   H         B   J   G   A   I
```

A. _E_ . It is a well _____ fact that George is a better student than Slim.

B. ____ . Slim had a _____ heart when Stacy left him.

C. ____ . This is a cleverly _____ cartoon.

D. ____ . When you are making the cake, add three well _____ eggs.

E. ____ . The police found the _____ car.

F. ____ . Ho Buom is a well _____ guy.

G. ____ . A college education helps people get well _____ jobs.

H. ____ . You should mend your _____ blouse.

I. ____ . Ice cream has more calories than _____ yogurt.

J. ____ . If you brag a lot, people will say you have a _____ head.

> The devil is said to have a *cloven* hoof. The verb forms are *cleave, cleft, cloven* or split as with an ax.

A. Swollen
C. Stolen
D. Torn
E. Known
I. Drawn
L. Paid
O. Built
S. Frozen
T. Broken
W. Beaten

© 1997 by The Center for Applied Research in Education

Intermediate ESL

2-58   WHO CAME LATELY: ADJECTIVES AND ADVERBS

Study the patterns and then answer the questions on the back of this sheet. The first one is done for you.

Patterns

1. Usually, adverbs are formed by adding *ly* to adjectives.
   She has a beautiful voice. She sings *beautifully*.

2. However, the following adjectives and adverbs have the same form:
   Early   Fast   Far
   Late   Hard

3. The adverbial form of *good* is *well*.

4. *Slow* and *loud* are sometimes used as both adjectives and adverbs, though sometimes *ly* is used to form adverbs.
   Correct: He runs slow. He speaks loud.
   Correct: He runs slowly. He speaks loudly.

5. How does a girl with a sweet voice sing? *She sings sweetly*.

© 1997 by The Center for Applied Research in Education

1. How does a fast runner run? <u>He/She runs fast.</u>

2. How does a good writer write?

3. How does an intelligent person speak?

4. How does a happy baby laugh?

5. How does a wise man speak?

6. How does an interesting speaker speak?

7. How does a hard worker work?

8. When does an early riser rise?

9. When does a late student get to class?

10. How does a heavy person walk?

11. If you walk to a far place, where do you walk?

12. How does a witty person speak?

"How does a sloppy
dresser dress?"
"Sloppily."

Name_____   Date_____

2-59   WHO DRIVES "FASTLIER":
COMPARISON OF ADVERBS

Study the rules. Then place the letters of the correct answers in the blanks before the sentences. Transfer the letters to the numbered blanks below. If your choices are correct, you will learn how to solve the following problem: How can you arrange the numbers 1, 2, 3, and 6 so that they will total 1?

Regular Adverbs	well, better, best
Pedro runs quickly.	fast, faster, fastest
Juan runs more quickly.	far, farther, farthest or further, furthest
Slim runs the most quickly.	late, later, latest
Irregular adverbs	early, earlier, earliest
bad, worse, worst	hard, harder, hardest

$$\underset{8}{\_}\ \underset{7}{\_}\ \underset{2}{\_} \qquad \underset{4}{\_}\ \overset{A}{\underset{1}{\_}}\ \underset{6}{\_}\ \underset{3}{\_} \quad + \quad \underset{11}{\_}\ \underset{4}{\_}\ \underset{9}{\_}\ \underset{2}{\_}\ \underset{2}{\_}$$

$$\underset{10}{\_}\ \underset{5}{\_}\ \underset{12}{\_}\ \underset{11}{\_}\ \underset{4}{\_}\ \underset{10}{\_} \quad = \quad 1$$

_____ 1. Slim runs __A__ than George.

(A) faster, (B) more fast, (C) fastlier

_____ 2. Slim works _____ than George.

(D) carelessly, (E) more carelessly, (F) carelesslier

_____ 3. A rabbit moves _____ than a turtle.

(E) rapider, (F) more rapidly, (G) more rapider

_____ 4. Mrs. Sikand came to the party _____ than Mr. Sikand.

(H) earlier, (I) more earlier, (J) early

_____ 5. George speaks _____ than Slim.

(G) intelligenter, (H) intelligently, (I) more intelligently

_____ 6. Yuko writes English _____ than Yoko.

(J) gooder, (K) goodlier, (L) better

_____ 7. Rosa studies _____ than Maria. hardly

(M) hardly, (N) harder, (O) more

© 1997 by The Center for Applied Research in Education

2-59 WHO DRIVES "FASTLIER" *(CONTINUED)*

_____   8. Ho Buom came to the football
               game _____ than Hasook.

_____   9. George plays tennis _____.

_____   10. Mrs. Sikand speaks _____ than
               Mr. Sikand.

_____   11. Stacy asked Slim to call her

               _____.

_____   12. She came to class _____
               than Gregor did.

(N) more lately, (O) later,
(P) latelier

(R) badly, (S) bad, (T) worse

(Q) most interesting, (R) more
interesting, (S) more interestingly

(R) soonly, (S) sooner, (T) soon

(V) more early, (W) early, (X) earlier

© 1997 by The Center for Applied Research in Education

© 1997 by The Center for Applied Research in Education

Name_____   Date_____

2-60 Dad Is Tied Up at the Office: Present and Past Passive

Study the passive patterns. Circle the letter beside the correct passive form of each active sentence. Then transfer the circled letters to the grid below. If your choices are correct, you will spell three words that read the same both across and down.

Patterns

1. The present passive is formed with *am, is, are* plus the past participle. The object of the active sentence becomes the subject of the passive.
   Active: I see a bird.
   Passive: A bird is seen.

2. The past passive is formed with *was* or *were* plus the past participle. Again the object of the passive sentence becomes the subject of the passive.

1a T	1b	1c
2a	2b	2c
3a	3b	3c

1a. *I saw a man.*
   S.   A man saw me.
   T.   A man was seen. *(circled)*
   U.   A man is seen.

2b. *A car hits a tree.*
   A.   A tree is hit.
   B.   A tree was hit.
   C.   A car hit a tree.

3c. *A woodcutter chopped down a tree.*
   C.   A tree is chopped down.
   D.   A woodcutter chops down a tree.
   E.   A tree was chopped down.

1b. *We sang a lot of songs.*
   E.   A lot of songs were sung.
   F.   A song was sung.
   G.   A lot of songs are sung.

2c. *Bob throws a fast ball.*
   S.   Bob threw a fast ball.
   T.   A fast ball is thrown.
   U.   A fast ball was thrown.

2a. *Farmers grow much corn in the Midwest.*
   C.   Much corn was grown.
   D.   Farmers were grown.
   E.   Much corn is grown.

3b. *A speeding car injured a man.*
   T.   A man was injured.
   U.   A man is injured.
   V.   A car is injured by a man.

1c. *The rock broke the window.*
   A.   The window was broken.
   B.   The window is broken.
   C.   The rock was broken.

3a. *The police officer saw the robber.*
   Z.   The robber is seen.
   A.   The robber was seen.
   B.   The police officer was seen.

BONUS QUESTION: What is the meaning of the idiom "tied up"?

131   **Advanced ESL**

2-61 BY AND BY: THE USE OF *BY* IN THE PASSIVE

Change the active sentences below to passive. Use *by* phrases as needed. The first one is done for you.

Active: A stray dog bit the child.
Passive: The child was bitten by a stray dog.

By phrases are used when they contain important information:
Romeo and Juliet was written by William Shakespeare.

The *by* phrase in the following sentence *doesn't* contain important information:
Much tea is imported from China by various importers.

© 1997 by The Center for Applied Research in Education

1. Oliver Stone directed the movie *JFK*.

   <u>The movie *JFK* was directed by Oliver Stone.</u>

2. Some construction workers built the bridge in 1990.

   _____

3. Many farmers grow corn in the Midwest.

   _____

4. William Shakespeare wrote *Romeo and Juliet*.

   _____

5. Thomas Edison invented the electric light bulb.

   _____

6. A thief at the beach stole my portable cassette player.

   _____

7. Our mail carrier delivered the package at 6:00.

   _____

8. The President delivered the speech.

   _____

9. Some construction workers built our house in 1985.

   _____

10. My grandfather designed his house.

    _____

2-62 HE'LL BE SPREAD TOO THIN: FUTURE AND PRESENT PERFECT PASSIVE

Study the patterns. Then write the passive form for each active sentence. The first one is done for you.

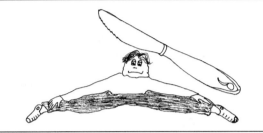

Active: He will eat sushi tomorrow night.
Passive: Sushi will be eaten.
Active: He is going to eat sushi tomorrow night.
Passive: Sushi is going to be eaten.

Active: He has eaten all the candy.
Passive: All the candy has been eaten.

1. The soldiers will surround the enemy camp.
   <u>The enemy camp will be surrounded.</u>

2. The fisherman will probably catch lots of fish.
   _____

3. The soldiers are going to surround the enemy camp.
   _____

4. The police have arrested the criminals.
   _____

5. Voters are going to elect two senators from each state.
   _____

6. The electrician has fixed the lights.
   _____

7. The newscaster will give the weather report at 10:00.
   _____

8. The critic is going to review the movie.
   _____

9. A masked gunman has robbed the bank.
   _____

10. The thief is going to steal the jewelry.
    _____

BONUS QUESTION: What is the meaning of the idiom "be spread too thin"?

© 1997 by The Center for Applied Research in Education

2-63   I "Oughta" Go Now: Modal Auxiliaries

Place appropriate modal auxiliaries in the sentence blanks. Then put numbers and letters of modal auxiliaries beside the sentences. Next transfer the letters beside each answer in order to the blanks below these directions. If your choices are correct, you will answer the following riddle: *What did the light bulb say to the pretty girl?*

Y
— — —   — — — —   — —   — —.

Modal Auxiliaries

1. (O) can, be able to
2. (N) can't, unable to, not able to
3. (U) could
4. (U) may, might

5. (O) must, have to, have got to
6. (N) don't have to
7. (Y) must not
8. (M) may I, can I, could I

9. (R) will you, can you, could you, would you
10. (E) ought to
11. (T) must (strong possibility)

---

1. The Bible says we M U S T   N O T kill. (7 Y)

2. John is talented. He _ _ _ swim, ski, sing, and dance. (__ __)

3. Gregor _ _ _ _ _ go to college in September. He isn't sure. (__ __)

4. Maria has a test tomorrow. She isn't at home studying. She _ _ _ _ be studying in the library. (__ __)

5. When I was in Colorado, I _ _ _ _ _ ski everyday. (__ __)

6. Tadeusz asked Mr. Sikand, "_ _ _ _ _   _ _ _ explain this problem?" (__ __)

7. I want to go to a movie tonight, but I'm _ _ _   _ _ _ _   _ _ because I have to take care of my younger sister. (__ __)

8. "_ _ _   _ please use your telephone?" (__ __)

9. Stacy wants ice cream for dessert, but she knows she _ _ _ _ _   _ _ eat a low calorie dessert. (__ __)

10. I have a test tomorrow, and I _ _ _ _   _ _ _   _ _ study. (__ __)

11. Slim said to Stacy, "If you're tired of me, you _ _ _'_   _ _ _ _   _ _ see me again." (__ __)

BONUS QUESTION: What is the meaning of the slang idiom in the answer to the riddle?

© 1997 by The Center for Applied Research in Education

2-64 He Must Have Forgotten: Three Uses of *Must*

Classify the uses of *must* by circling the letter in the appropriate column. Then record the letters in order on the blanks. If your choices are correct, you will explain the following situation: Yuko and her family got a new phone number when they moved. As Information wouldn't have this number for a few days, Yuko wrote her number on a piece of paper and gave it to Toshi. He promised to call her that night. But he didn't. Yuko was very angry. What do you think happened?

He M
___ ___ ___ ___   ___ ___ ___ ___   ___ ___ ___ ___ the phone number.

Uses of *must*

Necessity: I *must* go now.
Prohibition: You *must not* eat so much candy.

Strong possibility: Yuko has an exam tomorrow. She isn't at home studying. She *must be* at the library.

	Prohibition	Necessity	Strong possibility
1	(M)	A	R
2	U	B	S
3	V	S	C
4	W	T	T
5	H	U	D
6	I	A	D
7	J	V	E
8	K	W	E
9	L	X	F
10	M	O	G
11	N	O	S
12	O	T	H

1. High school kids must not smoke. Smoking is addictive.
2. Slim knows he mustn't call Stacy when she's studying.
3. I must do twenty algebra problems tonight.
4. Stacy won't answer the telephone when Slim calls. She must be mad at him.
5. You mustn't park in front of a fire hydrant.
6. Kids must go to school till they're sixteen.
7. Teachers must explain material so students can understand it.
8. Yuko goes out with Toshi every night. She must be in love.
9. The Ten Commandments say we must not steal.
10. The Ten Commandments say we must love our neighbors.
11. Mrs. Sikand didn't come today. She must be sick.
12. I really must stop eating so much chocolate.

© 1997 by The Center for Applied Research in Education

2-65 IF THE CAT'S AWAY, THE MICE WILL PLAY: PRESENT-FUTURE CONDITIONAL PATTERN

Study these present-future conditional patterns and complete the sentences in your own words.

> **Patterns**
>
> If I *eat* too much, *I'll get* fat.
> If I *make* a lot of money, *I'll buy* a car.

1. If I earn a lot of money this summer, _____.
2. If my parents say it's okay, _____.
3. If I don't study for my test, _____.
4. If it rains on Saturday, _____.
5. If a beautiful girl sits next to me in ESL, _____.
6. If the teacher gives too much homework, _____.
7. If I win the lottery, _____.
8. If I go to Hawaii, _____.
9. If I go to my grandmother's house for dinner, _____.
10. If I go to Disneyland this summer, _____.
11. If a robber breaks into my house, _____.
12. If there are tornado warnings, _____.
13. If I see a ghost, _____.
14. If I go to the most expensive restaurant in town, _____.
15. If the weather is hot and sunny this weekend, _____.

© 1997 by The Center for Applied Research in Education

2-66   A LAND OF MILK AND HONEY: MORE CONDITIONAL PATTERNS

Read the new conditional patterns. Then answer the questions in your own words. Write your answers on the back of this sheet.

---

1. If I *were* Queen of England, I *would* live in Buckingham Palace.
2. If I *lived* in Japan, I *might* learn to like raw fish.
3. If I *were* in Aspen, Colorado, I *could* go skiing everyday. (*Could* is past of *can*.)
4. If I *lived* in Aspen, Colorado, I *would be able to* go skiing everyday.

A.   What would you be able to do if you had a million dollars?

B.   What would you do if you were entirely alone in a department store?

C.   What would you do if you had magic power?

D.   What would you do if you found a robber in your home?

E.   What would you do if you saw a ghost?

F.   What would you do if a movie star asked you out?

G.   What would you eat if you were at a restaurant in your native country?

H.   What would you dream if you could choose your dreams?

I.   What would you do if you were President of the United States?

J.   What would you be able to do if you were an astronaut?

If we lived in a land
of milk and honey, we
wouldn't have any need
for money.

© 1997 by The Center for Applied Research in Education

2-67   WHICH DOCTOR?: CONDITIONAL REVIEW

Choose the correct word for each sentence blank. Write the letter of the word in the sentence blank. Then transfer the letters to the numbered spaces below these directions. If your choices are correct, you will answer the following question: There are two doctors in the small western town of Mud. One is healthy and strong. The other is sickly and weak. If you need a doctor in Mud, which one should you see?

__ __ __   __ __ C __   __ __ __ __ __ __
10 4 3   9 5 1 6   2 7 1 10 7 8

1. If I _____ high grades, my parents will be happy.
   ((C)) get, (D) will get

2. If I _____ enough money, I would buy a new car.
   (C) would have, (D) had

3. I wouldn't cut class if I _____ you.
   (E) were, (F) was

4. If you _____ in Japan last year, I would have taken you to Tokyo.
   (G) were, (H) had been

5. If I _____ in New York this summer, I will go to the
   (I) am, (J) were

   Museum of Modern Art.

6. If I swam well enough, I _____ enter the state competition.
   (K) would be able to, (L) can

7. If I eat too much fatty food, I always _____ weight.
   (N) have gained, (O) gain

8. If I _____ the Queen of England, I would live in Buckingham
   (Q) was, (R) were

   Palace.

9. If I lived in a land of milk and honey, I _____ have any need for money.
   (S) wouldn't, (T) didn't

10. If my father were wealthy, he _____ buy us anything we wanted.
    (S) will, (T) would

BONUS QUESTION: Why should you choose the doctor you did?

© 1997 by The Center for Applied Research in Education

2-68   PIE IN THE SKY: PRESENT WISHES

Read the patterns for present wishes. Then write a wish for each situation described below.

> **Patterns**
>
> Present wishes use past tense verbs.
>
> a. I wish I *were* Queen of England.
>   (In wishes, *were* is used with all persons.)
> b. I wish John *weren't* sick.
> c. I wish I *liked* vegetables.
> d. I wish I *didn't like* candy.
> e. I wish there *were* pie in the sky.
> f. I wish there *weren't* so many poor people in the world.

1. Tadeusz can't speak English well.

    _____

2. I have lots of problems.

    _____

3. I don't dance well.

    _____

4. I cry easily.

    _____

5. Yuko and Yoko look alike.

    _____

6. Slim is tall and thin.

    _____

7. Slim doesn't have a Jaguar.

    _____

8. Boris has a bad complexion.

    _____

9. Tod doesn't get high grades.

    _____

10. Li can't visit Taipei this summer.

    _____

11. Natasha can't get a date with Gregor.

    _____

12. Mr. and Mrs. Sikand don't own their own home.

    _____

BONUS QUESTION: What is "pie in the sky"?

© 1997 by The Center for Applied Research in Education

2-69 A FEW DOLLARS AND A LITTLE CASH: COUNT AND NON-COUNT NOUNS

"Count" nouns like *dog* or *dogs* can be counted. "Non-count" nouns like *mail* or *furniture* can't. We can say two dogs, but not two mail or two furniture. Place as many of the words as you can from the list below under each noun.

A	Several	A few	Many
An	Some	A lot of	Much
The	Two	A little	

Money
The
Some
A lot of
A little
Much

Dollar

Dollars

Furniture

Chair

Chairs

Apple

Apples

Things

Stuff

Salt

Jewelry

© 1997 by The Center for Applied Research in Education

SECTION THREE

STRUCTURE

3-1   OUCH: ONE-WORD SENTENCES

The sounds below show strong feelings. They are written with an exclamation point (!). Place the correct sounds beside each picture.

1. Darn!	(annoyance)	7. Ouch!	(pain)
2. Heck!	(annoyance)	8. Ow!	(pain)
3. Ick!	(disgust)	9. Ugh!	(disgust)
4. Nuts!	(annoyance)	10. Whoops!	(small accident)
5. Oh!	(surprise)	11. Wow!	(admiration)
6. Oops!	(small accident)	12. Whoopee!	(pleasure; excitement at a party)

A.

D.

B.

E.

C.

F.

© 1997 by The Center for Applied Research in Education

Name_____   Date_____

3-2   LOVE HIM OR LEAVE HIM:
IMPERATIVE SENTENCES

Test your skill in giving orders. Put the correct verb in each blank. In the imperative sentence, the subject is understood.

#			Verbs
1.	__Hurry__	up!	*Verbs*
2.	_____	the movie.	Be
3.	_____	the clock!	Beware
4.	_____	the door!	Close
5.	_____	your own business!	Do
6.	_____	care of yourself.	Don't be
7.	_____	up your clothes!	Eat
8.	_____	your horses!	Enjoy
9.	_____	for me!	Follow
10.	_____	me!	Hang
11.	_____	your shoes.	Have
12.	_____	your face!	Hold
13.	_____	out!	Hurry
14.	_____	careful!	Leave
15.	_____	of the dog!	Love
16.	_____	the window!	Mind
17.	_____	your homework!	Open
18.	_____	Chapter Six.	Read
19.	_____	your neighbor.	Stop
20.	_____	a good sport.	Take
21.	_____	your dinner!	Tie
22.	_____	fun.	Wait
23.	_____	me alone!	Wash
24.	_____	afraid.	Watch
25.	_____	thief!	Wind

© 1997 by The Center for Applied Research in Education

Name _____   Date _____

3-3 THE HYENA LAUGHED:
SUBJECT AND VERB SENTENCES

On the back of this sheet write two subject-verb sentences for each picture. You may use present, present progressive, past, or future sentences.

Model

The hyena laughs.
The hyena is laughing.
The hyena laughed.
The hyena will laugh.
The hyena is going to laugh.

1.

Gregor

2.

George

3.

Yuko

4.

Natasha

5.

Tadeusz

6.

Hans and Boris

© 1997 by The Center for Applied Research in Education

3-4   THE CAT IS FAT: SUBJECT, BE, ADJECTIVE

Write two sentences for each picture using the subject-be-adjective pattern. Use the back of this sheet for your answers.

Model	*Adjectives*	
Cat	confused	sick
	flat	silly
The cat is fat.	foolish	sloppy
The cat is important.	ill	strange
	odd	thoughtful
	puzzled	untidy
	round	wise

1.

Hat

2.

Rick

3.

Owl

4.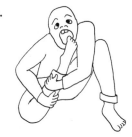

Nerd

5.

Morton

6.

Creature

© 1997 by The Center for Applied Research in Education

3-5 MO IS A MONSTER: SUBJECT, BE, NOUN

Use the subject-be-noun pattern to write sentences for each picture on the back of this sheet. Use *a, an,* and *the* as needed, but no other sentence parts.

Model	
Mo	
Mo is a monster.	

Nouns	
bat	friends
bird	money
coward	pet
door	sport

1.

Ho Buom, Slim, and Stacy

2.

Ice hockey

3.

The king

4.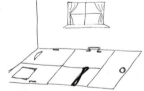

The floor

5.

The hat

6.

Coins

7.

A cat

© 1997 by The Center for Applied Research in Education

3-6   MAGIC WHEEL: SUBJECT, VERB, OBJECT

How many subject-verb-object sentences can you make with the words on the magic wheel? You may use any verb tense, but only three sentence parts: subject, verb, object. The sentences can be serious or funny, but not impossible. The student who makes the most sentences in fifteen minutes is the winner. Use the back of this page to write your sentences.

Models

The mouse is eating the cheese.
The mouse is going to eat the cheese.
The mouse is going to bite Slim.

The mouse ate the cheese.
The mouse might eat the cheese.
NOT: The cheese is going to eat the mouse.

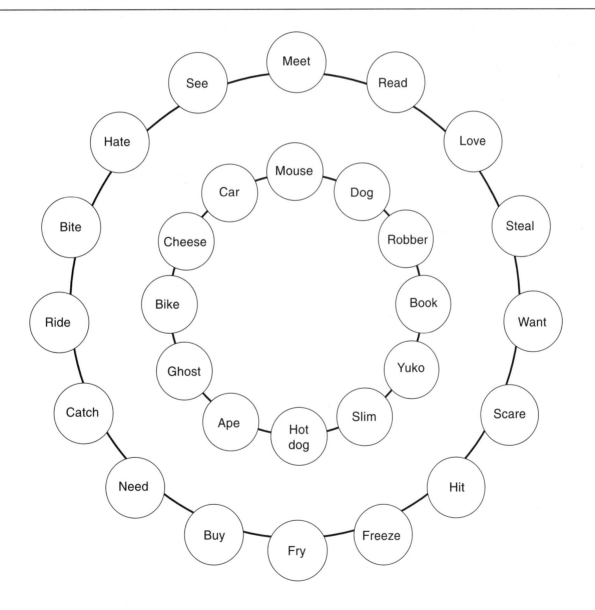

© 1997 by The Center for Applied Research in Education

Intermediate ESL

3-7 THEY FIGHT AT NIGHT: SUBJECT, VERB, PHRASE

Use the verbs and phrases below to write one sentence for each picture on the back of this sheet. Follow the subject-verb-phrase pattern. Do not use other sentence parts. Use any tense.

Model

They fight at night.
They are fighting at night.
They fought at night.
They'll fight at night.
They're going to fight at night.

Verbs	*Phrases*
	about a Jaguar
dream	beside Stacy
grow	on a rocking chair
jump	on a hat
sit	on trees
	over the moon
	with Natasha

1.

Slim, Stacy

2.

Slim

3.

The horse

4.

The cow

5.

Money

© 1997 by The Center for Applied Research in Education

Name _____ Date _____

3-8 A Girl and a Car: Subject, Verb, Object, Adjectival Modifier

Adjectives and adjective phrases help you paint word pictures. Use the modifiers from the list below or from your own imagination to make the following sentences more interesting and vivid. Use the back of the sheet for your sentences.

Model

Basic sentence: The girl is driving a car.
Expanded sentence: The girl *with golden hair* is driving a *sleek, black* car.

Suggested adjectives		*Suggested adjective phrases*
beautiful	hideous	in a leather mini-skirt
black-eyed	magical	in a torn uniform
blonde	pale	wearing a long, black robe
brave	savage	wearing a pointed hat
cruel	sinister	wearing an orange dress
flaming	slender	with a broken arm
frightened	sobbing	with a golden saddle
golden	toothless	with dark sunglasses
	wild-eyed	with flat tires
		with shining red feathers
		with smashed windows
		with wild red eyes

1. *Basic sentence:* The girl is driving a car.

2. *Basic sentence:* The girl saw a bird.

3. *Basic sentence:* The boy saw a monster.

4. *Basic sentence:* The soldier rode a horse.

5. *Basic sentence:* The boy entered the house.

6. *Basic sentence:* The child met a stranger.

7. *Basic sentence:* The magician had a box.

© 1997 by The Center for Applied Research in Education

3-9   MAD MARY DROVE HER CAR INTO A BRICK WALL: SUBJECT, VERB, OBJECT, ADVERBIAL MODIFIER

Adverbial modifiers answer such questions about the verb as *how, when, where, why*. In the title sentence, *Mad Mary drove her car into a brick wall,* the phrase *into a brick wall* tells where Mary drove her car. The sentences below contain *both* adjectival and adverbial modifiers. Underline all adverbs and adverbial phrases. Place their circled letters in the blanks beside the sentences. If your choices are correct, you will spell four adverbs that do *not* end in *ly*. The first one is done for you. Be careful! Some sentences may not have any adverbial modifiers.

1. Lovely Leona drove furiously down the avenue.   F   A
2. Nerdy slowly put his big, right foot into his mouth. ____   ____
3. Weary Willy Wilson ran wildly.   ____
4. Sad Sara Sanders slipped and fell in the icy street. ____
5. The tall attractive girl sang beautifully.   ____
6. The small, shy, unpopular boy was lonely.   ____   ____
7. The enormous bee stung the man on his elbow.   ____
8. The angry, growling dog bit the robber on the leg.   ____
9. Angry Anna Anderson screamed at her baby brother.   ____
10. The girl sang softly.   ____
11. Every elephant ate leaves in the evening.   ____
12. Herman hardly understands his history assignment.   ____
13. Annie Abbott ate apples in the afternoon.   ____
14. Rita wrote a letter to Randy.   ____
15. Winnie took a leisurely walk.   ____
16. The burning sun reddens the sky at dawn.   ____

© 1997 by The Center for Applied Research in Education

3-10 HERE AND THERE: VERB-SUBJECT WORD ORDER

Sentences beginning with *here* and *there* follow a verb-subject word order. Circle the first letter of the simple subject of each sentence below. Place the circled letters in the numbered spaces on the grid. If your choices are correct, you will spell the names horizontally of seven top students. You will spell vertically in the shaded boxes the subject in which they excel. The first one is done for you.

1. There goes a rhino in the jungle.
2. Here comes an ape swinging from tree branches.
3. There is also a savage lion in the jungle.
4. Here comes a gorilla pounding his chest.
5. There goes an orangutang behind him.
6. Here comes a giraffe nibbling leaves high in the trees.
7. There are eight brightly colored peacocks watching him.
8. Here come a dozen raccoons chasing the peacocks.
9. There are no polar bears in the jungle.
10. However, there are dangerous reptiles sliding through the undergrowth.
11. Are there seals in the jungle? I don't think so.
12. Are there grasshoppers in the jungle?
13. Here is a wild rose.
14. Are there eagles in the jungle?
15. Look, here are some orchids.
16. Of course, there are many monkeys chattering in the trees.
17. There are enormous hippos swimming in muddy water.
18. Here comes an antelope running from a pursuing lion.

© 1997 by The Center for Applied Research in Education

3-11   I Gave My Mother to the Pencil: Indirect Objects

Sentences with indirect objects can be written in two different ways. Study the models. Then, on the back of this sheet, rewrite each sentence, using the alternative pattern. The first one is done for you.

> *Models*
>
> I gave the pencil to my mother.   My mother made cookies for us.
> I gave my mother the pencil.   My mother made us cookies.

1. I gave my mother the letter.
   <u>I gave the letter to my mother.</u>

2. I bought a balloon for my baby sister.

3. Slim gave Stacy flowers.

4. I gave the tomatoes to Gregor.

5. Slim threw the basketball to Tod.

6. Mrs. Yamaoto made supper for us.

7. Mr. Sikand teaches us algebra.

8. Ranjana showed us her sari.

9. Mrs. Rodriguez made us enchiladas.

10. Mr. and Mrs. Kim bought us dinner.

11. I bought my mom a Mother's Day present.

12. Mr. Lopez told a story to us about his childhood in Spain.

13. Mr. and Mrs. Sato made us Christmas tree ornaments out of origami paper.

14. Hans built a house of cards for his little brother.

© 1997 by The Center for Applied Research in Education

3-12   I'D RATHER GIVE THAN TAKE:
MORE PRACTICE WITH INDIRECT OBJECTS

Usually, sentences with indirect objects may be written in two ways.

I gave the book to my mother.	He bought a present for us.
I gave my mother the book.	He bought us a present.

But in some cases, only one pattern is possible.

He fixed the car for me.	He painted the room for me.
NOT: He fixed me the car.	NOT: He painted me the room.

Complete the sentences below. Underline the correct completing phrase. Then place the letter of the completion in the numbered slot. If your choices are correct, you will learn how to change GIVE to TAKE in four easy steps, changing one letter at a time.

G I V E   Change __I__ in GIVE to _____ in the second word.
                          1   2

_ _ _ _   Change _____ in the second word to _____ in the third word.
_ _ _ _   3   4

_ _ _ _   Change _____ in the third word to _____ in the fourth word.
_ _ _ _   5   6

                 Change the second _____ in the fourth word to _____ in the fifth word.
                                    7   8

1. Tod fixed (I) Slim's bike for him, (J) Slim his bike.

2. Rosa translated (A) Spanish poems for us, (B) us Spanish poems.

3. Gregor pronounced (U) us the Russian words, (V) the Russian words for us.

4. Stacy opened (S) her mother for the window, (T) the window for her mother.

5. Mr. Sikand answered (G) questions for us, (H) us questions.

6. The corner restaurant cashed (S) Boris a check, (T) a check for Boris.

7. Hans handed (T) the book to Gretchen, (U) the book for Gretchen.

8. My grandfather gave (J) a book for me, (K) a book to me.

© 1997 by The Center for Applied Research in Education

3-13   I'D RATHER HAVE A COLA:
EXPRESSING PREFERENCE

Study the patterns and answer the questions under each picture.

© 1997 by The Center for Applied Research in Education

> *Patterns*
> 1. Which do you like better, pizza or hamburgers?
>   I like pizza better than hamburgers.
> 2. Which do you prefer, pizza or hamburgers?
>   I prefer pizza to hamburgers.
> 3. Which would you rather eat, pizza or hamburgers?
>   I would rather eat pizza than hamburgers.
> 4. Where would you rather go, to San Francisco or New York?
>   I would rather go to San Francisco than New York.

1. Who would you rather go out with, Mo or Zo?

Mo    **Zo**

2. Who do you like better, Nerda or Polly?

Nerda    **Polly**

3. Which do you prefer, lemon meringue pie or pecan pie?

4. Where would you rather go, to New York or the Colorado Rockies?

5. Which do you prefer, archery or bowling?

3-14 THE MOST IMPORTANT PERSON IN THE WORLD: TAG QUESTIONS WITH AUXILIARIES

Read the patterns. Then shade the numbers of the correct sentences. If your choices are correct, you will learn the name of the most important person in the world.

Patterns

Li can swim, can't she?
Quiang can't swim, can he?
Tod should go, shouldn't he?
Boris shouldn't go, should he?
Ahmed has to go, doesn't he?
Murad doesn't have to go, does he?

1 M	2 Y	3 S
4 R	5 O	6 N
7 I	8 U	9 B
10 T	11 V	12 A

1. You can fly to New York, can't you?

2. We can't go on a picnic in the rain, can't we?

3. I don't have to take the test, do I?

4. People shouldn't smoke, should they?

5. I don't have to read Chapter 24, will I?

6. We have to write a term paper in this class, don't we?

7. We don't have to give an oral report, do we?

8. Slim has to buy Stacy a birthday present, does he?

9. Gregor has to take Spanish, doesn't he?

10. We should study tonight, shouldn't we?

11. We shouldn't go to a movie, should we?

12. They don't have to work after school, do they?

© 1997 by The Center for Applied Research in Education

3-15   ME, TOO: AFFIRMATIVE AGREEMENT

Study the patterns and the model. Then write sentences of agreement under each picture. The first one is done for you.

Patterns

I'm a student. Rosa is, too. **OR** So is Rosa.
Ho Buom was at the game. Hasook was, too. **OR** So was Hasook.
Murad drinks a lot of cola. Nisme does, too. **OR** So does Nisme.
Yuko drank tea. Yoko did, too. **OR** So did Yoko.
George can figure skate. Gloria can, too. **OR** So can Gloria.

Model

Zo   Mo   Zo is a monster.
Mo is, too. **OR** *So is Mo.*

1.

The cat was scared.

The dog _____.

OR _____.

2.

Gregor can type.

Gloria _____.

OR _____.

3.

Ho Buom lifts weights.

George_____.

OR _____.

4.

Hans and Masha danced together.

Slim and Stacy _____.

OR _____.

© 1997 by The Center for Applied Research in Education

Name_____   Date_____

3-16   COUNT ME IN: MORE AFFIRMATIVE AGREEMENT

Study the patterns and the model. Then write sentences of agreement under each picture.

Patterns
Li's eaten too much pizza. I have, too. **OR** So have I.
Slim has a ten-speed bike. Tod does, too. **OR** So does Tod.
I'll be in class tomorrow. Murad will, too. **OR** So will Murad.
Li is going to buy a notebook. Quiang is, too. **OR** So is Quiang.

Model

Stacy and Slim have broken up.
Ho Buom and Hasook have, too. **OR** *So have Ho Buom and Hasook.*

1.

Gretchen has a twin sister.

Yuko _____.

OR _____.

2.

Yuko'll buy a dress.

Yuko _____.

OR _____.

3.

Slim is going to study tonight.

George_____.

OR _____.

4.

Hans and Boris have laughed.

Jose _____.

OR _____.

© 1997 by The Center for Applied Research in Education

3-17   ME NEITHER: NEGATIVE AGREEMENT

Study the patterns. Then circle the letters of the correct answers. Transfer these letters to the correctly numbered square or squares in the grid. If your choices are correct, you will construct a puzzle made up of common two-letter words. The first one is done for you.

Patterns

I'm not a doctor. Neither is Hans. **OR** Hans isn't either.
I wasn't in class. Neither was Tod. **OR** Tod wasn't either.
I don't drink cola. Neither does Li. **OR** Li doesn't either.
I didn't finish my homework. Neither did Nisme. **OR** Nisme didn't either.

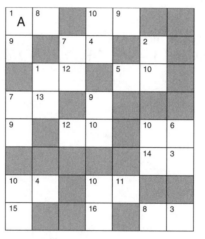

1. Rosa isn't a teacher. (A) Neither am I. (B) Either am I.
2. Pedro doesn't speak Russian. (C) Rosa can't neither. (D) Neither does Rosa.
3. They aren't Russian. (E) Neither are we. (F) Either do we.
4. I wasn't at the game. (F) Neither were they. (G) I haven't either.
5. Tadeusz didn't study. (F) Neither am I. (G) Neither did Slim.
6. I don't drink coffee. (G) Neither is he. (H) Neither does Hans.
7. Gloria doesn't like jazz. (I) Neither does George. (J) I do, too.
8. Hera doesn't drink coffee. (L) I do, too. (M) Neither does Li.
9. Li doesn't like beans. (N) Toshi doesn't either. (O) Walid also does.
10. Fyodor doesn't know how to dance. (O) Gary doesn't either. (P) I do, too.
11. I don't like sweet cakes. (R) Yuko and Yoko don't either. (S) Neither don't I.
12. Li wasn't in class. (S) Gregor wasn't either. (T) Neither did I.
13. Tadeusz isn't Canadian. (T) I'm not either. (U) Neither she is.
14. Nisme didn't come. (V) I didn't, too. (W) Walid didn't either.
15. Fen didn't read the book. (W) I don't either. (X) I didn't either.
16. Pedro doesn't eat sushi. (Y) Either does Rosa. (Z) Hans doesn't either.

© 1997 by The Center for Applied Research in Education

3-18   You're Not Going to Buy That Hat, Are You?: More Negative Agreement

Study the negative agreement patterns below. Then circle the letter of the correct expressions of negative agreement in sentences 1-6 that follow. Next, transfer the circled letters to the numbered spaces. If your choices are correct, you will learn how to change HATE to LOVE in three easy steps.

© 1997 by The Center for Applied Research in Education

> *Patterns*
>
> I won't go. Neither will I. **OR** I won't either.
> I'm not going to buy that crazy hat. Neither am I. **OR** I'm not either.
> I haven't eaten. Neither has he. **OR** He hasn't either.
> I don't have a car. Neither does he. **OR** He doesn't either.

Change ___T___ in HATE to _____ in the second word.
      1   2

Change _____ in the second word to _____ in the third word.
      3   4

Change _____ in the third word to _____ in the fourth word.
      5   6

H	A	T	E
—	—	—	—
—	—	—	—
L	O	V	E

1. Hasook won't marry Ho Buom,
   (T) will she? (U) won't she? (W) can she?

2. Slim doesn't have a Jaguar,
   (U) has he? (V) does he? (W) do they?

3. Rosa isn't going to work after school,
   (A) is she? (B) will she? (C) won't she?

4. You haven't seen Hans,
   (N) did you? (O) have you? (P) didn't you?

5. I'm not going to fail algebra,
   (G) will I? (H) am I? (I) aren't I?

6. Boris and George don't speak Polish,
   (J) can they? (K) does he? (L) do they?

"I'm not going to buy that crazy hat."
"Neither am I. I'm not either."

3-19   BOW-WOW: EMBEDDED QUESTIONS

Embedded questions are contained in answers to questions. Study the patterns, and match the questions and answers below. Write your answer letter next to each question. Then transfer the letters to the numbered spaces. Repeated numbers always equal the same letters. If your answers are correct, you will learn some "international dog language."

Patterns

Where is Slim?	I don't know where Slim is.
Where did Slim go?	I don't know where Slim went.
Are the keys lost?	I don't know if the keys are lost.
Were the keys lost?	I don't know if the keys were lost.

American dogs say: __ __ __ - __ __ __ or
                     6 5 3   3 5 3

__ __ __ __ - __ __ __ __
3 5 5 2   3 5 5 2

Chinese and Japanese dogs say: __ __ __ - __ __ __
                               3 4 7   3 4 7

German dogs say: __ __ __ - __ __ __
                 8 5 3   8 5 3

Russian dogs say: __ __ __ - __ __ __
                  8 4 1   8 4 1

_____ 1. Where is Li's dog?
_____ 2. Where was Li's dog?
_____ 3. Where did Li's dog go?
_____ 4. How did Li find her dog?
_____ 5. How did Li's dog get lost?
_____ 6. Is Li's dog lost?
_____ 7. When did Li's dog get lost?
_____ 8. Was Li's dog lost?

Using an embedded question,
give Hasook's answer to Ho
Buom's question, "Will you marry me?" Write
your answer on the back of this sheet.

A. I don't know how Li found her dog.

B. I don't know if Li's dog is lost.

F. I don't know where Li's dog was.

N. I don't know when Li's dog got lost.

O. I don't know how Li's dog got lost.

S. I don't know where Li's dog is.

V. I don't know if Li's dog was lost.

W. I don't know where Li's dog went.

© 1997 by The Center for Applied Research in Education

3-20   HE'S TOO SICK TO GO TO SCHOOL:
TOO AND *ENOUGH* WITH INFINITIVES

Both *too* and *enough* can be used before infinitives. *Too* is used with an affirmative or *yes* sentence; *enough* with a negative or *no* sentence. Study the examples. Then write the negative or *enough* pattern under each sentence. The first one is done for you.

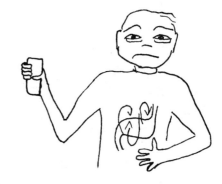

> ### *Examples*
> He is *too* ill to return to school.
> He isn't well *enough* to return to school.

1. He's too young to vote. (old)
   He isn't old enough to vote.

2. That suitcase is too heavy for me to carry. (light)

   _____

3. It's too late for us to go to the football game. (early)

   _____

4. He is too short to play basketball. (tall)

   _____

5. I'm too weak to lift a 100-pound weight. (strong)

   _____

6. She's too fat to wear tight jeans. (slim)

   _____

7. It's too cool for us to go swimming. (warm)

   _____

8. Her grades are too low for her to get on the honor roll. (high)

   _____

9. His vision is too poor for him to become a pilot. (good)

   _____

10. He is too unhappy to enjoy school life. (happy)

    _____

11. He is too irresponsible to take care of a pet. (responsible)

    _____

© 1997 by The Center for Applied Research in Education

3-21   HE MADE ME DO IT: CAUSATIVES—*MAKE, GET*

When causative verbs are used, the subject doesn't perform an action, but causes someone else to do it, as in "My mother made me study." Another causative pattern is "I got my watch fixed." First study the examples. Then read each sentence pair and circle the letter of the correct sentence. Put these letters in the numbered spaces in the grid to form six common words. The first one is done for you.

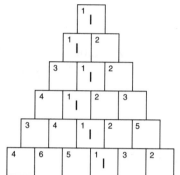

Examples

His mother made him
  take out the garbage.
His mother got him to take
  out the garbage.
He got his car repaired.

1.   (I)   He got his tooth filled.

   (B)   He got his filled tooth.

2.   (C)   His boss made him working overtime.

   (N)   His boss made him work overtime.

3.   (W)   The teacher made us to stay after school.

   (G)   The teacher made us stay after school.

4.   (R)   Ho Buom got us to go to the game.

   (P)   Ho Buom got us go to the game.

5.   (D)   He got his room paint.

   (S)   He got his room painted.

6.   (E)   The gym teacher made everyone do push-ups.

   (C)   The gym teacher made everyone doing push-ups.

He made me cry.

© 1997 by The Center for Applied Research in Education

3-22 LET ME BE: CAUSATIVES—*HAVE, LET*

When causative verbs are used, the subject doesn't perform the action; rather, it causes someone else to do it, as in "My mother had me take out the garbage." Other causative patterns are "He had the TV set fixed." "My mother let me go."Study the examples and place a check beside the *incorrect* sentences. Then write the circled letters found in the *incorrect* sentences in the numbered spaces below. If your choices are correct, you will answer the following riddle: WHY SHOULDN'T YOU TELL A FUNNY STORY WHILE YOU'RE ICE SKATING?

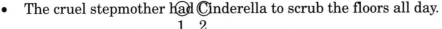

The __ __ __   __ __ __ __ __   __ __ __ __ __   __ __!
      6 2 3   8 6 4 5 11   2 10 1 2 7   12 9

> *Examples*
> The teacher had us read a story.
> The teacher let us pick our own topics.
> (*Let* = permitted or allowed)
> He had the oil in his car changed.

- The cruel stepmother had Cinderella to scrub the floors all day.
                            1   2
- My mother had me go to the store for bread.
  1   2
- We let the car warm up before we got in.
  3   4
- Mother had all the windows washing.
       3   4
- The teacher let the children to run around in the kindergarten room.
                        5   6   7
- The teacher let the children play with clay.
                             5   6
- Mr. Parker had us to do somersaults in gym.
       9   8
- My father had the lamp repaired.
             8   9   10
- My uncle had the broken window to repaired.
     12   11   10
- My mother had the fallen tree taken away.
               11 12

BONUS QUESTION: Can you explain the riddle? What is the meaning of the activity title?

© 1997 by The Center for Applied Research in Education

3-23   WHAT'S HIS NAME?:
NOUN CLAUSES AS SUBJECTS

Sometimes clauses are used as subjects and sometimes as objects. Study the examples and identify the sentences in the pairs that have clauses as *subjects*. Then transfer the circled letters in
subject clauses to the numbered blanks below. If your choices are right, you will answer the question in the verse that follows. The first one is done for you.

There was an elephant,
Happy and tame.
What would you say
Was the big beast's name?

$$\underset{9}{\_\_}\ \underset{3}{\_\_}\ \overset{A}{\underset{1}{\_\_}}\ \underset{7}{\_\_} \qquad \underset{9}{\_\_}\ \underset{5}{\_\_}\ \underset{8}{\_\_}\ \underset{4}{\_\_}\ \underset{2}{\_\_} \qquad \underset{10}{\_\_}\ \underset{5}{\_\_}\ \underset{8}{\_\_} \qquad \underset{6}{\_\_}\ \overset{A}{\underset{1}{\_\_}}\ \underset{10}{\_\_}$$

Examples of clauses as subjects:
What he said isn't important.
Who he is isn't important either.
What he does is important.

Examples of clauses as objects:
I don't care *what you wear*.
I'll like *whatever you choose*.
I'll go *where you want to go*.

---

1. I don't care wheth(e)r or not you buy a car. <u>Wh(a)t you do</u> is your business.

2. If she (c)omes, I'll be happy. What she's going to (d)o is uncertain.

3. (H)ow she'll come is not certain. We don't know i(f) she wants to come.

4. Whose (c)ar is this? When it was (l)eft in the street is a mystery.

5. If you (c)ome, I'll be home. Whatever y(o)u decide will be fine with me.

6. What he (s)aid wasn't clear. I don't know (w)hat he meant.

7. (I) think that the movie was funny. Why i(t) was funny is hard to explain.

8. (Y)ou won't pass if you don't study. How y(o)u study is also important.

9. (W)hy he's here doesn't interest me. I only know that he('s) here.

10. What (y)ou want is sometimes hard to get. I don('t) think that he likes me.

© 1997 by The Center for Applied Research in Education

Name_____   Date_____

3-24 I Don't Know Why I Love You: Noun Clauses as Objects

Sometimes clauses are objects of sentences. Study the examples. Then identify the underlined clause in each sentence as either an object or subject clause. Place the number *following* each sentence in the correct column. If your answers are correct, both columns will have the same total.

Objects	Subjects
A 5	
B	
C	
D	
E	
F	
G	
H	
I	
J	

Examples

Clause as subject: Why I love you is a mystery to me.
Clause as object: I don't know why I love you.

A. Everyone knows <u>that George is an honor student.</u> (5)

B. Do you understand <u>why Stacy broke up with Slim</u>? (4)

C. Does Hasook care <u>if Ho Buom decides not to go to college</u>? (3)

D. <u>Whether or not Ho Buom goes to college</u> doesn't interest me. (10)

E. <u>When you get to class</u> is your worry. (7)

F. I don't believe <u>that Stacy and Slim can be happy together.</u> (1)

G. I don't understand <u>why geometry is a required subject.</u> (5)

H. Don't ask me to guess <u>what the answer to that question is.</u> (2)

I. <u>Whatever you decide</u> is your business. (4)

J. All the kids wish <u>that Stacy and Slim wouldn't fight all the time.</u> (1)

© 1997 by The Center for Applied Research in Education

Intermediate ESL

3-25   I THINK SO: *SO* REPLACING NOUN CLAUSES

Sometimes *so* takes the place of a noun clause. Read the examples. Then write a noun clause for each picture on the back of this sheet that explains the meaning of *so*. The first one is done for you.

> **Examples**
>
> Does Slim love Stacy? I think so.
> So = I think that Slim loves Stacy.

1.

Does Ho Buom lift weights? I think so.
<u>I think that Ho Buom lifts weights.</u>

2.

Are owls wise? I think so.

3.

Do parrots understand what you say?
I think so.

4.

Does George know the answer to the
question? I think so.

5.

Do people imagine flying saucers?
I think so.

6.

Is Katya crying because Tadeusz
went away? I think so.

© 1997 by The Center for Applied Research in Education

3-26   OUT OF THIS WORLD: COMPOUND SENTENCES

Compound sentences often consist of two clauses joined by *and, but, for, or,* or *so.* Circle the correct joining word for each sentence. Copy the letters of the correct joining words in the numbered spaces below. The first one is done for you. If your choices are correct, you will answer the following riddle: HOW DO MEN FROM MARS DRINK COFFEE?

<table>
<tr><td>___</td><td>___</td><td>___</td><td>___</td><td>A
___</td><td></td><td>___</td><td>___</td><td>___</td><td>___</td><td>___</td><td>___</td><td></td><td>___</td><td>A
___</td><td>___</td><td>___</td><td>___</td><td>___</td></tr>
<tr><td>4</td><td>11</td><td>10</td><td>8</td><td>1</td><td></td><td>4</td><td>7</td><td>14</td><td>6</td><td>9</td><td>5</td><td></td><td>12</td><td>1</td><td>13</td><td>2</td><td>3</td><td>11</td></tr>
</table>

1. Slim is tall, _____ George isn't.
   (A) but, (B) and, (C) or

2. Slim likes Stacy, _____ Todd does, too.
   (A) but, (B) so, (C) and

3. Hasook dates Ho Buom, _____ she doesn't want to marry him.
   (D) and, (E) but, (F) or

4. Yuko might go to college in September, _____ she might work a year.
   (F) or, (G) but, (H) so

5. George gets good grades, _____ he studies hard.
   (E) or, (F) so, (G) for

6. Tod dates Yoko, _____ Toshi dates Yuko.
   (H) or, (I) and, (J) but

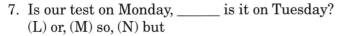

7. Is our test on Monday, _____ is it on Tuesday?
   (L) or, (M) so, (N) but

8. I was hot, _____ I took a cool shower.
   (K) or, (L) but, (M) so

9. Did Slim call Stacy, _____ or did Stacy call Slim?
   (N) or, (O) so, (P) for

10. It was cold and rainy, _____ we didn't have a picnic.
    (M) and, (N) but, (O) so

11. Would you like to go to a movie, _____ would you like to stay home?
    (R) or, (S) but, (T) and

12. Gregor studied for his algebra test, _____ he didn't get a good grade.
    (Q) and, (R) so, (S) but

13. Rosa is beautiful, _____ Maria is beautiful, too.
    (T) for, (U) and, (V) so

14. Toshi likes Yuko, _____ he asked her out.
    (W) or, (X) but, (Y) so

© 1997 by The Center for Applied Research in Education

Intermediate ESL

3-27   SLIM'S TALL, BUT STACY ISN'T:
COMPOUND SENTENCES—REVERSALS

In reversals, the meaning of the second sentence is opposite to the meaning of the first. Study the examples and complete each of the sentences below. You may make up all names, but they must be singular. The first one is done for you. Use the back of this sheet for your answers.

Examples

Slim is tall, but Stacy isn't
Stacy is short, but Slim isn't.
George went to Chicago, but Slim didn't.
Slim didn't go to Chicago, but George did.

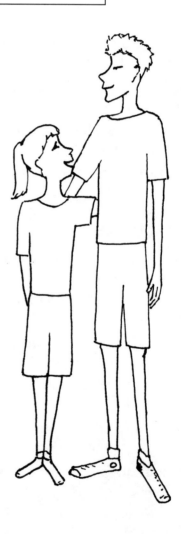

1. Gregor didn't study,   <u>but George did</u>.
2. Slim doesn't like sushi,
3. Ho Buom wants to go to the game,
4. Boris doesn't speak Spanish,
5. I'll be in New York tomorrow,
6. Slim won't get a high grade in algebra,
7. Yuko can't swim,
8. Slim has a 10-speed bike,
9. George has gone to many operas,
10. Maria went to Mexico City,
11. Mr. Sikand teaches algebra,
12. I have to study tonight,
13. Ahmed isn't a citizen,
14. I don't have a sports car,
15. I have never been to Ecuador,
16. I'll be going to the dance,
17. I won't get a high grade in history,
18. Mr. Sikand isn't from Bolivia,
19. Cats don't bark,
20. A fish isn't a mammal,
21. I couldn't do the hard assignment,
22. Yuko is going to buy a new coat,

© 1997 by The Center for Applied Research in Education

© 1997 by The Center for Applied Research in Education

Name _____   Date _____

3-28   UNTIL YOU CAME:
COMPLEX SENTENCES—SUBORDINATING CONJUNCTIONS

Place the correct subordinating conjunction in each sentence. Then place the subordinating conjunctions in the puzzle grid. If your choices are correct, you will be able to fit all the subordinating conjunctions below into the grid. The first one is done for you.

After	Before	Until
Although	If	When
As soon as	Unless	While

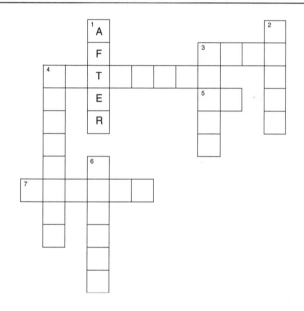

Down

1. <u>After</u> graduation, I'm going to get a job.
2. _____ I met my boyfriend, I was always lonely and unhappy.
3. The phone rang _____ I was doing my homework.
4. _____ I finish my homework, I'm going to watch TV.
6. _____ I go to sleep tonight, I'm going to write to my grandmother.

Across

3. Hasook wants to go to medical school _____ she graduates from college.
4. _____ he is short, he is a terrific basketball player.
5. _____ I don't keep my B average, I won't stay on the honor roll.
7. You won't pass history _____ you turn in a term paper.

Intermediate ESL

3-29   THE WONDERFUL WORLD OF THE FUTURE: COMPLEX SENTENCES—PRESENT-FUTURE PATTERN

The present-future pattern occurs with *if, when, after, before,* and *as soon as.* Study the examples. Then practice the pattern by completing the sentences below. The first two are done for you. Use your own ideas to complete the sentences.

> *Examples*
>
> Before I go to sleep, I'll do my homework.
> When I go to New York, I'll see a musical.
> After I finish high school, I'll get a job.
> As soon as I get home, I'll take a shower.
>
> OR
>
> I'll do my homework before I go to sleep.
> I'll see a musical when I go to New York.
> I'll get a job after I finish high school.
> I'll take a shower as soon as I get home.

After I graduate,
I'll go to the prom.

1. After I graduate from high school, <u>I'll go to college</u>.
2. <u>I'll go to college</u> after I graduate from high school.
3. When I get married, _____.
4. I'm going to have two children _____.
5. Before I go to college, _____.
6. _____ before I go to college.
7. If I met a perfect guy/girl, _____.
8. I will probably go steady for awhile _____.
9. When I get a job, _____.
10. _____ when I get a job.
11. If I go to Disneyland, _____.
12. _____ if I go to Disneyland.
13. After I finish my homework, _____.
14. _____ after I finish my homework.
15. When class is over, _____.
16. _____ when class is over.
17. If I get straight A's _____.
18. As soon as I get home _____.
19. _____ as soon as I get home.
20. I'll go iceskating _____.
21. I'll go to the beach _____.
22. When summer comes, _____.

© 1997 by The Center for Applied Research in Education

© 1997 by The Center for Applied Research in Education

Name_____   Date_____

3-30   WHICH COMES FIRST?:
COMPLEX SENTENCES WITH TIME CLAUSES

Decide if the action in the underlined clause occurs first or second. To indicate this, write *1st* or *2nd* after each sentence and put the sentence number in the correct column in the grid. If your choices are correct, the multiplied column totals will equal 750. The first one is done for you.

1st	2nd
1	

_____ X _____ = 750

1. Before Toshi ate dinner, <u>he watched Star Trek.</u>   1st

2. After Stacy talked to Slim, <u>she did her homework.</u> _____

3. <u>When Ho Buom got to the gym,</u> he lifted weights. _____

4. <u>I made cookies</u> before I cleaned my room. _____

5. <u>Gregor bought a candy bar</u> when he got to the school store. _____

6. When Zo walked into the grocery store, <u>everybody screamed.</u> _____

7. When the dog saw the cat, <u>he began to bark.</u> _____

8. The dog began to bark <u>after he saw the cat.</u> _____

9. Before it began to rain, <u>I ran home.</u> _____

10. <u>It began to rain</u> after I got home. _____.

Intermediate ESL

3-31 I'D REALLY LIKE TO:
COMPLEX SENTENCES WITH INCOMPLETE INFINITIVES

Sometimes, infinitive phrases are not completely expressed. First, read the examples. Then find the correct sentence in each group and circle the word in parentheses. Write this word above the correct number in the blank. The first one is done for you. If your choices are correct, you will write a well-known proverb. Can you explain it?

_____   _____   _____   _____   _____   _____
   5   2   6   4   3   8

hatched!

_____   _____
   7   1

Examples

I've never eaten sushi, but I'd like to.
I've never figure skated, but I want to.

---

1. (hatched))   I've never seen a purple cow, but I'd like to.
   (trees)   I've never gone to Paris, but I'd like that.
   (leaves)   I've never scuba dived, but I want.

2. (count)   I don't live in Singapore anymore, but I used to.
   (autumn)   Toshi didn't take Yuko to the dance, but he wanted to do.
   (flowers)   I took the test, but I didn't want.

3. (Dracula)   I've never believed in vampires, and I don't believe.
   (before)   I didn't believe in Santa Claus when I was a kid, but I wanted to.
   (after)   I don't have to go to the movies, but to school I have to.

4. (dream)   I never learned to play tennis, but I tried it.
   (hogs)   I've never gone to Paris, but I hope to.
   (chickens)   I haven't written my grandmother yet, but I'm going to.

5. (always)   I've never learned to ski, but I've tried.
   (don't)   Stacy asked, "Did Yoko enjoy the picnic?" I said, "She seemed to."

6. (your)   "Do you want to go to the game?" "Yes, I'd love to."
   (warm)   "Does Slim have a sports car?" "No, he doesn't to."

7. (under)   "I'm sorry I hurt your feelings. I didn't intend."
   (are)   The kids don't want to take the test, but they've got to.
   (is)   I've never learned to figure skate, but I have learned to.

8. (beside)   I won't study for the test, but I ought.
   (they)   I didn't learn to play chess, but I tried to.
   (him)   I didn't go, but I planned to go.

© 1997 by The Center for Applied Research in Education

3-32   LILA HAS A CAR:
COMPLEX SENTENCES WITH ADJECTIVE CLAUSES

Clauses beginning with *that, which, who,* or *whom* often describe nouns. First, study the models. Then, using the words in the boxes, describe Lila; then describe her car. The person who writes the most adjective clauses in ten minutes wins.

Models

Lila is a girl *who dislikes boys.*
Lila has a car *that looks expensive.*

A. Lila is a girl _____.

who	dislikes	a blonde wig	algebra	scary movies
	has	a boyfriend	a new car	school
	likes	a cat	a pet raccoon	
	wants	a date this	boys	
		Saturday	dancing	
		a diamond ring	hamburgers	

1. who has a diamond ring

2. _____

3. _____

4. _____

5. _____

6. _____

7. _____

8. _____

9. _____

10. _____

11. _____

12. _____

B. Lila has a car _____.

that	costs	a CD player	dented
which	has	a convertible top	pink
	is	a flat tire	rusty
	looks	a lot of money	shiny
		a musical horn	
		a powerful engine	

1. that has a CD player

2. _____

3. _____

4. _____

5. _____

6. _____

7. _____

8. _____

9. _____

10. _____

11. _____

12. _____

Intermediate ESL

© 1997 by The Center for Applied Research in Education

3-33   A SAD CAT: COMPLEX SENTENCES WITH MEDIAL ADJECTIVE CLAUSES

Sometimes, adjective clauses beginning with *that, which, who,* or *whom* are placed between subjects and verbs. Study the patterns below. Write sentences with medial adjective clauses under each picture. The first one is done for you. (Remember, *who, whom,* and *that* refer to people; *that* and *which* refer to things.)

Patterns

The steak was tough. *I had it for lunch.*   *I saw a bird.* It was pretty.
The steak *that I had for lunch* was tough.   The bird *that I saw* was pretty.

1.

I saw a cat. It looked sad.
<u>The cat that I saw looked sad.</u>

2.

The car was a convertible. Lila drove it.
_____
_____

3.

The girl was cute. Boris looked at her.
_____
_____

4.

Murad ordered soup. It had a fly in it.
_____
_____

5.

The fish was enormous. Gloria caught it.
_____
_____

6.

The student worried about the test.
He had a pile of books on his desk.
_____
_____

7.

The blouse had a dollar collar.
Yelina liked wearing it.
_____
_____

© 1997 by The Center for Applied Research in Education

3-34 DO WE REALLY WANT *THAT*?:
COMPLEX SENTENCES—THE USE OF *THAT*

When replacing objects, *that, who,* and *which* can be omitted in adjective clauses. Study the examples and identify the correct sentences below. Place the circled letters in each *correct* sentence in the numbered space in the puzzle grid. If your choices are correct, you will spell five separate words. One is done for you.

1 T	2 H	3 E	4	5
6				7
8	9	10	11	12
13				14
15	16	17	18	19

Examples

That replacing an object:
The puppy is cute. I petted *him.*
Correct: The puppy *that* I petted
 is cute.
Correct: The puppy I petted is cute.

That replacing a subject:
The box is on the table. *It* is heavy.
Correct: The box that is on the table
 is heavy.
Incorrect: The box is on the table is heavy.

A. Lila is a girl has many friends.
   (1)   (2)

B. This is the boy I met at Lila's party.
   (1)   (2)   (3)

C. Land is in Japan is expensive.
       (1) (2)   (3)

D. The student left early is Boris.
       (4)   (3)

E. I saw a cat I wanted to take home.
    (4)   (5)

Advanced ESL

3-34 Do We Really Want *That?* *(Continued)*

F. I met a student from Ethiopia I really liked.
                     (6)   (7)

G. The flowers are in the garden are beautiful.
    (6)   (7)

H. The student is singing is my girlfriend.
        (8)   (9)   (10)

I. Otto, who is from Germany, studied English at home.
   (8)   (9)   (10)

J. The guy Emi marries has to be intelligent.
   (11)   (12)   (13)

K. Many buildings are in New York are skyscrapers.
   (11)   (12)   (13)

L. People live in Brazil speak Portuguese.
   (14)   (15)   (16)

M. The city Yoko likes best is Denver.
   (15)   (14)   (16)

N. The gardens that are in Kyoto are lovely.
    (17)   (18)   (19)

O. The garden are in Kyoto are lovely.
   (17)   (18)   (19)

© 1997 by The Center for Applied Research in Education

© 1997 by The Center for Applied Research in Education

Name_____ Date_____

3-35   WHY IS LEONA'S HAIR STANDING ON END?: COMPLEX SENTENCES—BECAUSE

Study the patterns and write complex sentences with *because* under each picture. The word list will help you. Though one word can be used twice, some words can't be used at all.

> *Patterns*
>
> Why is Ho Buom strong?
> He's strong because he exercises.

Word List

afraid
clumsy
hot
famous
hungry
lazy
popular
sad
strong
stupid
thirsty
tired

1.

Why is Pedro perspiring?

_____

_____

2.

Why is Gloria drinking a cola?

_____

_____

3.

Why is Olaf tangled up in the net?

_____

_____

Advanced ESL

3-35 WHY IS LEONA'S HAIR STANDING ON END?
(CONTINUED)

4.

Why is the king hiding behind the throne?

_____

_____

5.

Why is Nerd putting his foot in his mouth?

_____

_____

6.

Why is Leona's hair standing on end?

_____

_____

© 1997 by The Center for Applied Research in Education

3-36 "DON'T BUY THAT TIE": REPORTED SPEECH—*NOT* PLUS INFINITIVE

Following the pattern in the model, report the speech for each picture on the back of this sheet. Replace *don't* with *not* plus *infinitive*.

> *Model*
>
> Mother told the children, "Don't eat so much candy."
> Mother told the children not to eat so much candy.

1.

The neighbors told the kids, "Don't make so much noise."

The neighbors told the kids not to make so much noise.

2.

I told my father, "Don't buy that tie."

3.

I begged the hunter, "Don't shoot the fox."

4.

I told the cashier, "Don't give me a lot of pennies."

© 1997 by The Center for Applied Research in Education

3-36 "DON'T BUY THAT TIE" (CONTINUED)

5.

The letter carrier told me, "Don't forget the stamps."

6.

I told Kahled, "Don't hit your finger with the hammer."

7.

Leona told her baby brother, "Don't get in my hair." (*annoy me*)

8.

Boris's mother told Boris, "Don't fall."

© 1997 by The Center for Applied Research in Education

Name_____ Date_____

3-37 "I'M DROWNING":
REPORTED SPEECH—PRESENT TENSE

Study the rules and the model. Then write reported speech under each picture. The first one is done for you.

> **Rules**
>
> Change verbs to the past tense.
> Use third person.
> **Note:** *That* can be omitted.

> *Model*
>
>
>
> **"I'm drowning."**
>
> *Murad said that he was drowning.* **OR** *Murad said he was drowning.*

1.

"I love you."

Slim said that he loved Stacy.

2.

"I think that dress is cute."
"I like it, too."

Yuko said _____

Yoko said _____

3.

"I'm broke."
(*broke* = without money)

Slim said _____

© 1997 by The Center for Applied Research in Education

3-37   "I'M DROWNING" *(CONTINUED)*

4.

"I'm going to turn a somersault."

Gregor said _____

5.

"I don't want any pizza."

Emilio said _____

6.

"I don't feel well."

Boris said _____

7.

"There's a fly in my soup."

Arthur said _____

© 1997 by The Center for Applied Research in Education

3-38 "I Cried Last Night": Reported Speech—Past Tense

Study the model and the rules. Then write reported speech under each picture.

Model

"I cried last night."

Natasha said that she had cried last night.

Negative: "I didn't cry over Gregor." Natasha said *that* she hadn't cried over Gregor.

Rules

Use third person.
Change past verb to the past perfect (*had* plus past participle).

Change *you* to *I* or *me*.
Negative: "I didn't hear you." John said that he didn't hear me.

1.

"I studied until 2:00 A.M."

Slim said _____

2.

"I drilled a hole in the tree."

The woodpecker said _____

3.

"I had a great dinner."

Mr. Jones said _____

© 1997 by The Center for Applied Research in Education

3-38   "I Cried Last Night" *(Continued)*

4.

"I pulled up a telephone pole."

Bo said _____

5.

"I didn't hear you."

Funny Bunny said _____

6.

"I ate a hamburger."

The octopus said _____

7.

"We were cold."

The ice mice said _____

© 1997 by The Center for Applied Research in Education

3-39   "I WON'T HURT YOU": REPORTED SPEECH—FUTURE TENSE

Study the rules and the model. Then write reported speech under each picture.

Rules

Use the third person.
Change *will* to *would*.
Change *you* to *I* or *me*.

Model

"I won't hurt you."

The dentist said that he wouldn't hurt me.

© 1997 by The Center for Applied Research in Education

1.

"I'll fix your leaking pipe."

The plumber said _____

2.

"We'll win the game."

Big Hunk said _____

3.

"I'll land safely."

Masha said _____

3-39 "I Won't Hurt You" (Continued)

4.

"I'll hit a homer."

Tadeusz said _____

5.

"We'll dance until dawn."

Gregor and Natasha said _____

6.

"I'll walk on the moon."

The astronaut said _____

7.

"I'll take a good picture of you."

Gretchen said _____

© 1997 by The Center for Applied Research in Education

3-40 "THAT'S SILLY": REPORTED SPEECH—ASSORTED TENSES

Part I: Place the letters of reported speeches beside the correct quotations. Then transfer these letters to the numbered spaces below. If your choices are correct, you will learn three slang words Americans use to describe something silly.

2	5 A	6	3	10
7	1	6	6	10
4	9	8	8	10

"That's silly."

__A__ 1. Slim said, "I'm fine."	E. Slim said (that) he would be fine.
_____ 2. Slim said, "I was fine."	O. Slim said (that) he could go.
_____ 3. Slim said, "I'll be fine."	P. Slim said (that) he might go.
_____ 4. Slim said, "I'm going to be fine."	T. Slim said (that) he had gone.
_____ 5. Slim said, "I can go."	Y. Slim said (that) he might be fine.
_____ 6. Slim said, "I may go."	A. Slim said (that) he was fine.
_____ 7. Slim said, "I must go."	S. Slim said (that) he had to go.
_____ 8. Slim said, "I went."	N. Slim said (that) he was going to be fine.
_____ 9. Slim said, "I'll go."	U. Slim said (that) he would go.
_____ 10. Slim said, "I may be fine."	D. Slim said that he had been fine.

Part II: Write the reported speech under each picture.

1.

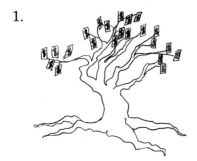

Slim said, "Money grows on trees."
Report Stacy's disagreement.
Stacy said

_____

_____

2.

Murad said, "I have to hit the books." (*have to study*)
Murad said

_____

_____

© 1997 by The Center for Applied Research in Education

SECTION FOUR

PRONUNCIATION

4-1   RED HEAD /ĕ/: SOUNDS AND SYMBOLS

Study the phonetic symbols below and write the correct vowel symbol beside each word. These symbols will help you use the *American Heritage Dictionary* and many other dictionaries.

Symbols			
/ă/	as in bad	/ŏ/	as in hot
/ā/	as in ate	/ō/	as in no
/ĕ/	as in bed	/ou/	as in cow
/ē/	as in meet	/ŏŏ/	as in good
/ĭ/	as in sit	/ōō/	as in boo
/ī/	as in hi		

1. beat __ē__

2. believe _____ _____

3. bend _____

4. bite _____

5. blow _____

6. break _____

7. breath _____

8. buy _____

9. cab _____

10. cable _____

11. cake _____

12. cat _____

13. coat _____

14. each _____

15. eight _____

16. field _____

17. fight _____

18. float _____

19. food _____

20. fry _____

21. grow _____

22. head _____

23. height _____

24. heat _____

25. how _____

26. instead _____ _____

27. loud _____

28. me _____

29. meat _____

30. meet _____

31. mood _____

32. neighbor _____

33. receive _____ _____

34. shoe _____

35. shoot _____

36. should _____

37. though _____

38. tie _____

39. vote _____

40. wood _____

© 1997 by The Center for Applied Research in Education

© 1997 by The Center for Applied Research in Education

Name_____   Date_____

4-2   A BAD BED: SHORT /Ă/ AND /Ĕ/

Can you hear the difference between /ĕ/ in *bed* and /ă/ in *bad*? Test your ability to hear these sounds. Your teacher will read one word from each pair below. Circle the word you hear.

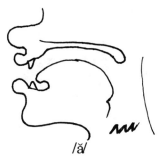

/ă/

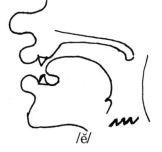

/ĕ/

a bad bed

1. ad, Ed
2. am, Em
3. and, end
4. ax, ex
5. bad, bed
6. bag, beg
7. ban, Ben
8. band, bend
9. bass, Bess
10. bat, bet
11. Brad, bread
12. brat, Brett
13. can, Ken
14. dad, dead
15. Dan, den
16. gas, guess
17. hack, heck
18. had, head
19. ham, hem
20. hat, Het

21. lad, led
22. lag, leg
23. land, lend
24. mad, med
25. man, men
26. mass, mess
27. mat, met
28. pack, peck
29. pan, pen
30. pat, pet
31. rack, wreck
32. sad, said
33. Sal, sell
34. sand, send
35. sat, set
36. Tad, Ted
37. tan, ten
38. than, then
39. vast, vest
40. vat, vet

Intermediate ESL

Name_____ Date_____

4-3 A BAT IN A VAT: /B/ AND /V/

Asian languages don't have the English /v/ sound. This activity will test your ability to hear the difference between /v/ and /b/. Your teacher will choose one word in each pair and read it to you. Circle the word you hear.

/v/   /b/   **a bat in a vat**

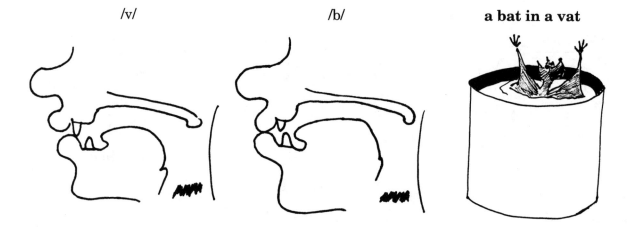

Initial / b / and / v /

1. ballad, valid
2. ban, van
3. banish, vanish
4. bat, vat
5. bend, vend
6. best, vest
7. bet, vet
8. beer, veer
9. berry, very
10. box, vox
11. base, base
12. Beale, veal
13. beep, veep
14. bile, vile
15. boat, vote
16. bolt, volt
17. bowel, vowel

Medial / b / and / v /

1. cabs, calves
2. rabble, ravel
3. ebb, Ev
4. Gibb, give
5. slob, Slav
6. dub, dove
7. hub, of
8. Serb, serve
9. curb, curve
10. curbing, curving
11. jibe, jive
12. fiber, fiver
13. lobes, loaves
14. robe, rove
15. globe, grove
16. cube, you've

© 1997 by The Center for Applied Research in Education

4-4   I HOPE YOU ENJOY YOUR FLIGHT: /L/ AND /R/

Part I: As Asian languages do not have the English /r/ sound, many Asian newcomers will not hear the difference between words like *fright* and *flight*. This activity will test your ability to hear the difference between /l/ and /r/ sounds. Your teacher will read one word in each pair. Circle the word you hear.

Initial sounds

1. race, lace
2. rate, late
3. ray, lay
4. read, lead
5. red, led
6. rice, lice
7. right, light
8. rip, lip
9. row, low
10. wrap, lap
11. wrong, long

Medial sounds

12. cram, clam
13. freeze, fleas
14. fright, flight
15. fruit, flute
16. grew, glue
17. Irene, Eileen
18. pray, play
19. steering, stealing

Final sounds

20. fire, file
21. poor, pool
22. steer, steal
23. tire, tile
24. tore, tall

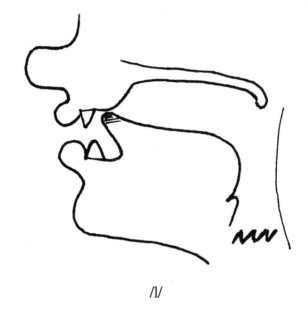

/l/

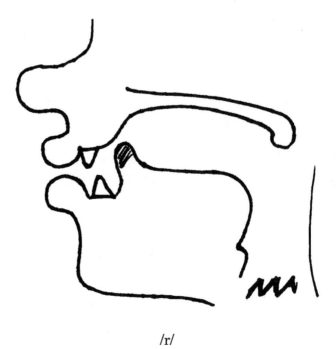

/r/

© 1997 by The Center for Applied Research in Education

4-4 I HOPE YOU ENJOY YOUR FLIGHT *(CONTINUED)*

Part II: Write the correct words under each picture.

A.

_____

B.

_____

C.

_____

D.

_____

E.

_____

F.

_____

Word list
flight
flute
fright
fruit
lip
rip

© 1997 by The Center for Applied Research in Education

© 1997 by The Center for Applied Research in Education

Name_____   Date_____

4-5   MR. SCHICK IS VERY SICK: *SI* AND *SHI*

The Japanese, Chinese, and Korean languages have a *shi* sound that is easily confused with the English *si* as in *sit* or *sip*. Can you hear the difference between words like *sip* and *ship*? You will find out as your teacher reads one word from each pair and you circle the word you hear.

Initial sounds

1. sick, Schick
2. sickle, Shickle
3. sieve, shiv
4. sift, shift
5. sill, shill
6. simmer, shimmer
7. sin, shin
8. Sinbad, shin pad
9. single, shingle
10. sip, ship
11. sir, shir
12. siv, shiv
13. six, Schick's

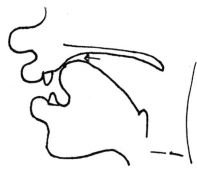

/s/

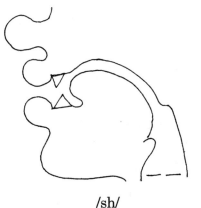

/sh/

Medial sounds

14. cussing, Cushing
15. gassing, gashing
16. leasing, leashing
17. massing, mashing
18. messing, meshing
19. miss again, Michigan
20. pursuing, Pershing

Final sounds

21. Cass, cash
22. crass, crash
23. furnace, furnish
24. muss, mush
25. pumice, punish

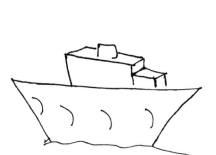

This is a *ship*.

Gloria is going
to *sip* a soda.

4-6   SOME THUMB: /s/ AND /TH/

Can you hear the difference between /s/ as in *some* and /th/ as in *thumb*? You'll find out when you score this activity. Your teacher will read one word in each pair. Circle the words you hear.

Initial sounds

1. sank, thank

2. sick, thick

3. sin, thin

4. sing, thing

5. sink, think

6. some, thumb

7. seem, theme

8. sigh, thigh

9. saw, thaw

10. sought, thought

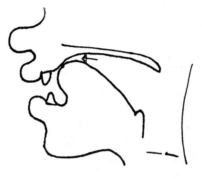

/s/

Medial sounds

11. tense, tenth

12. lessen, lengthen

13. worse, worth

14. truce, truth

15. face, faith

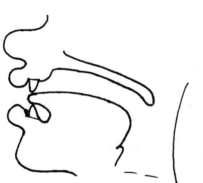

/th/

© 1997 by The Center for Applied Research in Education

4-7   TWO MOUTHS, TWO TEETH: /TH/ AND /*TH*/

Learning the difference between /th/ in *think* and /*th*/ in *they* may be difficult for you because Chinese, Japanese, French, and Italian do not have these sounds. To help you hear them, your teacher will read the list below. Write each word in the correct column. Be sure to copy the letter beside each word into the column, too. The first one is done for you. If your answers are correct, the letters you've copied will spell two new *th* words in each column.

/th/

/*th*/

two mouths, two teeth

Word list

T	thought
T	them
H	thing
H	weather
O	thunder
E	either
U	thank you
I	other
S	teeth
R	leather
A	thief
W	than
N	bath
E	those
D	with
A	they
S	thought
T	leather
O	through
H	another
U	thief

/th/ as in think

Letter	Word
T	thought

/*th*/ as in they

Letter	Word

© 1997 by The Center for Applied Research in Education

Name_____ Date_____

4-8 "THE RAIN IN SPAIN FALLS MAINLY IN THE PLAIN": LONG /ā/

Circle all words (from the word list) in the grid that have the long /ā/ sound. The words may be vertical (up and down) or horizontal (across). Then write the names of the pictures below and circle the letters that spell the long /ā/ sound.

T	A	T	M	H	T	H	E	H	F
H	N	O	R	A	I	N	B	A	R
E	T	F	A	T	T	E	O	B	E
Y	E	A	O	E	O	I	U	I	I
I	F	T	P	I	C	G	Q	T	G
T	A	E	E	T	A	H	U	M	H
S	S	A	N	G	B	B	E	A	T
L	A	B	O	R	L	O	T	N	O
I	V	O	H	A	E	R	E	Y	E
H	E	A	E	Y	A	S	A	P	E

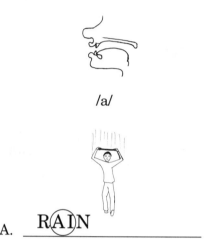

/a/

A. R(AI)N_____

B. _____ C. _____ D. _____ E. _____

Word list

ape	freight (train)	labor	they
ate	gray	neighbor	yea
bouquet	hate	rain	
cable	save		

© 1997 by The Center for Applied Research in Education

4-9   THE MANY FACES OF EVE: LONG /Ē/

The long /ē/ sound is spelled in various ways. Choose words from the list below that have the long /ē/ sound and fit into the grid. If you place these words in the grid correctly, the shaded spaces will spell a word that has two long /ē/ sounds and a final silent *e*.

/ē/   **sheep**

beak	breath	free	president
bee	breathes	grief	receive
bite	dead	hate	spread
bitten	even	head	the
bled	flower	led	then
bleed			

B

E

A

R

Intermediate ESL

© 1997 by The Center for Applied Research in Education

4-10   OUR TEAM'S AHEAD:
LONG AND SHORT /E/ SOUNDS

Some *ea* words have the long /ē/ sound as in *sea*. Others have the short /ĕ/ sound as in *head*. When the listed words below have the long *e* sound, put the letters beside them in the long /ē/ column. When words have the short *e* sound, put the letters beside them in the short /ĕ/ column. If your choices are correct, you will spell two new long and short *e* words in the correct columns. Record the letters in order.

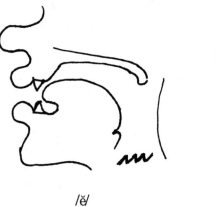
/ĕ/

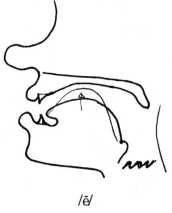
/ē/

/ĕ/ head	/ē/ eat
B	P

P. mean

B. bread

R. thread

E. cream

A. grease

N. steal

E. head

A. healthy

K. wealthy

U. weak

F. instead

A. dead

T. leak

S. meat

S. deaf

T. weather

© 1997 by The Center for Applied Research in Education

© 1997 by The Center for Applied Research in Education

Name_____   Date_____

4-11   HI, I WANT TO BUY A TIE: LONG /ī/

Circle the new long /ī/ words hidden in the sentences. The first one is done for you (my). Then write the names of the pictures and circle the letter or letters that spell the long /ī/ sound.

1. "Boom boom," Yelina said loudly.

2. "Don't sigh," Tom said.

3. Abu Hemen isn't from an Arab country.

4. All I ever said to him was said kindly.

5. If I've hurt you, I'm sorry.

6. "Crack it, even though it's a thick piece of wood."

7. Dick indicated that he was tired.

8. "Rob, I keep thinking that you're angry with me."

9. "David, Yelina is talking to you."

10. It emerged from the deep water.

11. His English is terrific.

12. Mr. Hym eats onions.

13. If I reserve the book, no one else can take it.

14. I centered the flowers on the table.

15. "Jim, Indians were in America before Europeans."

/ī/

A.

_____

B. _____

C.

_____

D.

_____

E.

_____ _____

Word List	
ice mice	guy
tie	fry
pie in the sky	

4-12   HELLO, JOE, WHAT DO YOU KNOW?: LONG /ō/

This activity will help you remember the different letters that are pronounced as long /ō/. Place the various long /ō/ words in the grid below, guided by clue letters and word length.

Across

coke	oat
goat	okay
hello	old
hole	slow
home	though
no	

Down

cloaks	note
coal	oh
elbow	ow
go	so
hoe	yoyo
mole	

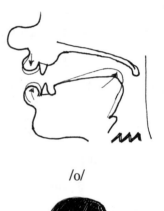

/o/

Nose

© 1997 by The Center for Applied Research in Education

© 1997 by The Center for Applied Research in Education

Name _____   Date _____

4-13   DO YOU KNOW JOE BLOW?: *OW* AS LONG /ō/

Sometimes the letters *ow* have the sound of long /ō/ as in *slow*. First, circle all *ow* words with the long /ō/ sound in the sentence below. Then write the correct *ow* words under each picture. Be careful! Some sentences may not have any long /ō/ *ow* words!

/ō/

1. Do you (know) Joe (Blow) from a little town called King's Crown?
2. The crows flew slowly over the yellow tower.
3. "Wow," said the sow, "that's a pretty big cow."
4. She took a bath when the water power ran so low she couldn't shower.
5. Flowers might not grow in shadows or in snow.
6. Don't fall down in the river and drown.
7. Now that you're grown, you might have known the tall grass needs to be mown.
8. In Japan, polite people bow. We wrap packages with a pretty bow.
9. In school, children sit in rows. When people fight, they have rows.
10. The mother said, "Now, don't throw snow. You know better than that."

A.

The hot sun _____s.

D.

Did you _____ the ball through the window?

B.

_____ing is a sport.

E.

This package has a pretty _____.

C.

The girls are _____ing.

Word List	
bow	rowing
bowling	throw
glows	

4-14   A BROWN OWL: *OW* AS /ou/ OR /ō/

Sometimes *ow* has the sound of /ō/ as in *slow* and sometimes the sound of /ou/ as in *cow*. Put the number beside each list in the correct column. If your answers are correct, the total of the numbers in the /ō/ column will double the total of the numbers in the /ou/ column.

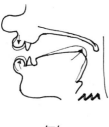

/ō/

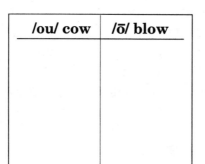

/ou/ cow	/ō/ blow

TOTALS: _____ _____

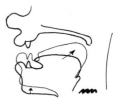

/ou/

© 1997 by The Center for Applied Research in Education

1. owl
    fowl
    growl
    howl
    towel
    vowel

2. owe

3. blow
    low
    slow

4. cow
    how
    now

5. clown
    down
    frown
    grown

6. There is no 6!

7. crow
    grow
    row

8. show
    snow
    throw

9. bowl

10. brown
    crowd
    drown

11. arrow
    fellow
    yellow
    window

owl

4-15   MR. BROWN WENT TO TOWN:
THE SOUNDS OF *OW* AND *OU*

This activity provides practice in recognizing *ow* and *ou* pronounced as /ou/ in *cow*. In the sentences below, circle all words with the /ou/ sound. Be careful!

cow

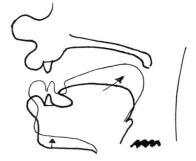

/ou/

1. "Where are you now?" said the farmer to the cow.
2. Don't go out in the snow before I plow.
3. The wind is blowing the rows of flowers.
4. I ought to tell you about a tough guy named Mr. Stout.
5. Even though George did the paper out of class, he got through with his work without difficulty.
6. Mr. Brown went to town to buy his daughter a flowered gown.
7. I know you have a bad cough, but don't shout at me.
8. Father frowned as the snow drifted through the open window.
9. The dogs are howling and growling.
10. Mom said, "I bought six new towels, but I still don't have enough."
11. Why are you scowling at me?
12. Walking south, he opened his mouth and thought about the house he bought.
13. "It's rough," she said with a cough as she sat on the bough.
14. If her mother allows her, she'll wear lipstick and powder.
15. Slim said, "Grow up! Or don't you know how?"
16. Is an owl a fowl?
17. During the show, did the clown fall down in front of the crowd?
18. It's a bit low to owe so much dough (money) to your own brother.
19. The crow said, "Caw." The cat said, "Meow." The dog said, "Bow wow." Mom said, "Now now."
20. They fought about who brought the fish they bought.

Intermediate ESL

© 1997 by The Center for Applied Research in Education

4-16   HE CAN'T GET HIS FOOT IN THE BOOT: LONG AND SHORT /oo/

Long /o͞o/ has the sound of *oo* as in boot. Short *oo* has the sound of /o͝o/ as in book. Test your ability to recognize these sounds by completing the fill-ins below.

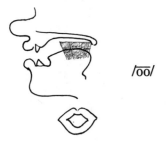
/o͞o/

/o͝o/

© 1997 by The Center for Applied Research in Education

/o͞o/ boot

1. He talks <u>t</u>OO much.
2. A horse's foot: _OO_.
3. Top of a house: _OO_.
4. Not warm: _OO_.
5. We swim in a _OO_.
6. We sit on a _ _OO_.
7. Thread is wound around a _ _OO_.
8. We eat _OO_.
9. The train whistle went "_OO_-_OO_."
10. In spring, flowers _ _OO_.
11. A loud noise is a _OO_.
12. We sweep the floor with a _ _OO_.
13. The opposite of rich is _OO_.
14. We eat soup with a _ _OO_.
15. At night the _OO_ comes out.
16. Twelve P.M. is _OO_.

/o͝o/ book

1. the opposite of bad is _OO_.
2. The past tense of stand is _ _OO_.
3. _OO_ comes from trees.
4. The past tense of shake is _ _OO_.
5. Twelve inches is a _OO_.
6. To see is to _OO_.
7. Another word for stream is a _ _OO_.
8. A dishonest person is a _ _OO_.
9. Sheep give us _OO_.
10. We catch fish with a line and a _OO_.
11. The past tense of understand is _ _ _ _ _ _OO_.
12. Something that isn't straight is _ _OO_ed.
13. The past tense of take is _OO_.
14. A small, cozy space is a _OO_.
15. Is your mom a good _OO_?

4-17 RICE IS NICE: SOFT *c* SOUND /s/

Sometimes *c* has a hard sound /k/ as in *cat*. Other times, *c* has a soft sound /s/ as in *city*. Put words with the soft *c* or /s/ sound in the grid below. Word lengths and clue letters will help you. If your choices are correct, you will spell a new word in the shaded spaces. This word begins with soft *c* sound /s/ and names an insect with a hundred legs.

/s/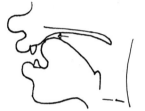

advice	cattle	counter	decide
bicycle	cent	cousin	Mac
cabs	city	cube	nice
cane	clothes	cute	price
cape	cloud	dance	prince
carrot			

© 1997 by The Center for Applied Research in Education

Name_____ Date_____

4-18 CARL CAN'T COME: HARD *c* SOUND /k/

Sometimes *c* has the hard sound of /k/ as in *cat, cowboy,* and *unicorn.* Find words in the list that have the hard *c* sound. Copy the circled letters in these words in the blanks below. If your choices are correct, you will spell the answer to this riddle: What word is wrong when you pronounce it right?

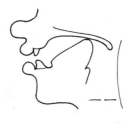

/k/

W __ __ __ __

1. ⓝice

2. priⓒe

3. centeⓡ

4. cenⓣ

5. croⓦn

6. ⓑounce

7. prinⓒe

8. citⓨ

9. caⓡrot

10. faⓒe

11. ⓡace

12. ⓟencil

13. clⓞud

14. ⓢpace

15. priⓝcipal

16. ⓟlace

17. caⓝ

18. centⓤry

19. iⓒe

20. recoⓖnize

21. ⓓecide

22. cereⓜony

23. Ciⓝcinnati

24. citiⓩen

25. adⓥice

cat

cowboy

unicorn

© 1997 by The Center for Applied Research in Education

Name_____ Date_____

4-19 GET SOME KNOWLEDGE IN COLLEGE: SOFT AND HARD *G* SOUNDS

Sometimes *g* has the soft sound of /j/ as in *change* and sometimes it has the hard sound of /g/ as in *girl*. Decide if the words below have the soft or hard *g* sounds. Blacken the letters in the grid that precede the words with the *hard sound* /g/ as in grid. If your choices are correct, you will divide the grid into five equal sections.

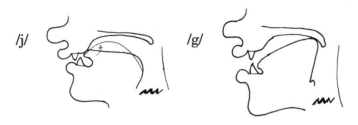

A.	girl	F.	goose	K.	garden	P.	forgive	U.	go
B.	bag	G.	give	L.	age	Q.	bug	V.	hug
C.	glad	H.	change	M.	begin	R.	forget	W.	grow
D.	ago	I.	ground	N.	cigarette	S.	goat	X.	orange
E.	get	J.	game	O.	danger	T.	college	Y.	grab

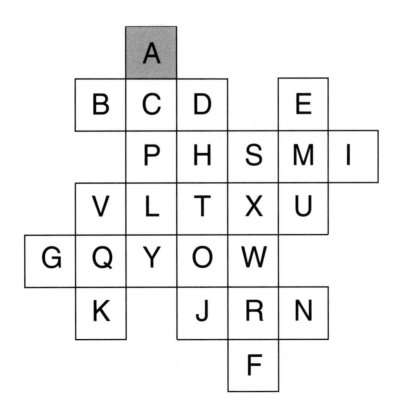

© 1997 by The Center for Applied Research in Education

Intermediate ESL

4-20   A BEAR IN THE AIR: *R*-CONTROLLED VOWELS

Do you know how to pronounce words with *r*-controlled vowels that may have varying spellings but the same sound? Test yourself by finding rhymes in the list for each of the words below.

A. *are /ä/*

   1. _____caviar_____

   2. _____

   3. _____

   4. _____

B. *air /â/*

   1. _____

   2. _____

   3. _____

   4. _____

   5. _____

   6. _____

C. *here /ĭ/*

   1. _____

   2. _____

   3. _____

   4. _____

   5. _____

D. *or /ô/*

   1. _____

   2. _____

   3. _____

   4. _____

E. *fur /û/*

   1. _____

   2. _____

   3. _____

| care |
| caviar |
| dear |
| deer |
| far |
| floor |
| here |
| jar |
| near |
| pier |
| purr |
| rare |
| roar |
| sir |
| star |
| store |
| their |
| there |
| they're |
| tore |
| we're |
| were |
| where |

Bear in the air

© 1997 by The Center for Applied Research in Education

4-21   A GHASTLY GHOST: SILENT LETTERS

From the list below, choose ten words that have silent letters. Copy the words. Write their silent letters to the right and their circled letters to the left. The first one is done for you. If your choices are correct, the circled letters will spell two other words that have silent letters.

Circled letters	*Words*	*Silent letters*
1. g_____	wrong_____	w_____
2. _____	_____	_____
3. _____	_____	_____
4. _____	_____	_____
5. _____	_____	_____
6. _____	_____	_____
7. _____	_____	_____
8. _____	_____	_____
9. _____	_____	_____
10. _____	_____	_____

Word list

ⓓog	pⓝeumonia
wronⓖ	lunⓒh
tⓗough	nⓞte
presidⓔnt	baⓓ
gⓞat	ⓜean
Ⓢoap	happ(y)
siⓝg	rⓔceive
knoⓣt	riⓒh
tⓗat	morninⓖ
knowinⓖ	prⓘncess

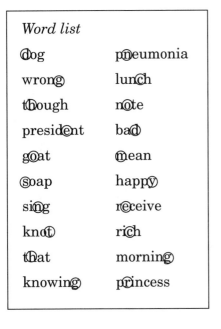

© 1997 by The Center for Applied Research in Education

4-22   "It's Rough," She Said with a Cough as She Sat on the Bough: Like and Unlike Pronunciations

Sometimes vowel sounds in words are spelled alike, but have different pronunciations, like the *ow* in *cow* and *slow*. Sometimes vowel sounds in words are spelled differently but have the same pronunciation like the long /ā/ sound in *ate* and in *neighbor*. If the words in the pairs below have the same vowel sounds, put their letters in the column marked "same." If the vowel sounds are different, put the letters in the column marked "different." If your answers are correct, you will have a baker's dozen in each column. (A baker's dozen is thirteen.)

same	different
A	

_____   _____

A. bead, bread
B. through, bough
C. lie, buy
D. food, good
E. eight, ate
F. heal, heel
G. hole, goal
H. lost, most
I. freeze, peas
J. shoe, toe
K. bear, pair
L. boot, foot
M. ought, caught
N. sea, see
O. instead, Ted
P. guy, my
Q. wool, fool
R. though, cough
S. dead, red
T. rough, thorough
U. laugh, giraffe
V. low, how
W. door, bore
X. grow, plow
Y. cow, mow
Z. could, shout

© 1997 by The Center for Applied Research in Education

Name_____   Date_____

4-23   PLEASE SNEEZE:
SAME PRONUNCIATION, DIFFERENT SPELLINGS

Many rhyming words in English are spelled differently. Can you match the words on the left with their rhymed mates on the right? Put the numbers of the rhyming words in the blanks.

A. I, _23_, _29_, _32_, _42_, _50_
B. laugh, ____
C. there, ____, ____, ____
D. bite, ____, ____
E. please, ____, ____
F. most, ____
G. choose, ____, ____, ____, ____, ____, ____, ____
H. do, ____, ____, ____, ____
I. head, ____, ____
J. loud, ____
K. off, ____
L. nose, ____, ____, ____, ____
M. box, ____
N. size, ____, ____, ____
O. pain, ____, ____
P. green, ____, ____

Q. lied, ____, ____, ____
R. learn, ____, ____
S. taught, ____
T. say, ____, ____
U. hate, ____, ____
V. leave, ____
W. oh, ____, ____, ____
X. are, ____
Y. cow, ____, ____

1. bait
2. bean
3. bees
4. blue
5. blues
6. bough
7. bought
8. car
9. clocks
10. clothes
11. cough
12. crews
13. cries
14. crowd
15. cruise
16. dyed
17. eyes
18. fair
19. fern
20. fight
21. freight
22. froze
23. fry
24. Gene
25. giraffe
26. go
27. grieve
28. grows
29. guy

30. height
31. hey
32. hi
33. hide
34. Jane
35. knew
36. lose
37. reign
38. rise
39. said
40. scare
41. shoes
42. sigh
43. sighed
44. slow
45. sneeze
46. tear
47. Ted
48. thou
49. through
50. tie
51. toast
52. toe
53. toes
54. turn
55. use
56. views
57. weigh
58. you

His nose grows
down to his toes.

213   Advanced ESL

4-24   THE RABBIT HABIT: A SHORT VOWEL PATTERN

Vowels have a short sound when single consonants or consonant blends come before or after single vowels in words or syllables. Some examples are *sad, cash, slap,* and *basket.* Sometimes the consonant or consonant blend comes only *after* the single vowel as in *at, am,* or *ash.* Find a place in the grid for all words in the list with short vowels. If your choices are correct, you will spell a new short vowel word in the shaded, vertical spaces. This new word is the name of a sport that is played with a shuttlecock.

believe	dive	mint
bend	fantastic	planting
besides	fine	receive
bicycle	heat	rode
blanket	Joe	sadness
camel	like	shopping
coat	meat	thank

© 1997 by The Center for Applied Research in Education

4-25   I Hate Your Hat: Magic *e*

When an *e* is added to one-syllable words ending in a vowel-consonant, the vowel changes from short to long and the *e* is silent. *Hat,* for example, becomes *hate.* Try to identify the words below that change in meaning through addition of a final *e*.

1. A small rug: M <u>A</u> <u>T</u>
   A husband or wife: M <u>A</u> <u>T</u> <u>E</u>

2. Something that can hold two pieces of cloth together: P__ __
   An evergreen tree: P__ __ __

3. Opposite of lose: W__ __
   Something to drink: W__ __ __

4. A part of a fish: F__ __
   When you feel well, you feel F__ __ __.

5. The dog B__ __ the man.
   The dog is going to B__ __ __ the man.

6. Something you do with scissors: C__ __
   If a girl is pretty, guys say she's C__ __ __.

7. A lot of noise: D__ __
   Another word for eat: D__ __ __

8. Short form of a girl's name: M__ __.
   This book is M__ __ __.

9. A white metal: T__ __
   A part of a fork: T__ __ __

10. Slender: SL__ __
    A thick, unpleasant liquid: SL__ __ __

11. To intend to do something: PL__ __
    You fly in a PL__ __ __.

12. Not brightly lit: D__ __
    Ten pennies: D__ __ __

13. If you want a cat or dog to go away, you might say: SC__ __
    You do this with roller blades or on ice: SK__ __ __

I hate your hat.

© 1997 by The Center for Applied Research in Education

4-26 PEOPLE LIVE THEIR LIVES:
PRONUNCIATION OF FINAL *S* AS /s/ OR /z/

Part I: In plurals and in singular verbs, *s* is pronounced /z/ after the voiced sounds—*b, d, g, l, m, n, r, v, oy,* and *ay*. For example, we say one dog and two dog*z*. *S* is pronounced /s/ after unvoiced sounds—*k, p, t*. For example, we say hat*s*, not hat*z*. Shade the letters in the grid for words from the word list with a final /s/ sound and circle the word itself. The first one is done for you. If your choices are correct, the remaining letters will spell a popular proverb. Can you explain it? Use the back of this sheet for your answer.

W	B	A	C	L
L	D	S	P	N
A	F	G	V	E
E	A	I	R	J
K	M	S	N	O

These are twin*z*, not twin*ce*.

Part II: Write the plurals of each of the words in the pictures below. Circle the correct sound of the final *s*.

A. cabs
B. (cooks)
C. desks
D. soups
E. heads
F. cups
G. looks
H. walls
I. bats
J. books
K. socks
L. balls
M. clocks
N. rocks
O. pots
P. tops
R. beds

S. boys
V. plays
W. lives

1._____   /s/, /z/

2._____   /s/, /z/

3._____   /s/, /z/   4._____   /s/, /z/

© 1997 by The Center for Applied Research in Education

Name _____   Date _____

4-27   HUH?: /ə/ IN UNACCENTED SYLLABLES

Vowels in unaccented syllables have the sound of *uh* like *a* in *above*. Dictionaries show this sound with the following symbol /ə/ which is called a schwa. You can test your knowledge of words with unaccented syllables in this activity. Twenty words are broken into two parts. The first part of the word is in column one; the second, in column two. Put the broken words together. Place the letters from column two beside the beginning parts in column one. Next, write the complete word and circle all vowels that have the schwa or *uh* sound.

/ə/

Huh?

Column one

1. a __A__ ____I____
2. a ____ _____
3. al ____ _____
4. ap ____ _____
5. aw ____ _____
6. beau ____ _____
7. com ____ _____
8. de ____ _____
9. differ ____ _____
10. en ____ _____
11. exer ____ _____
12. fa ____ _____
13. intel ____ _____
14. mis ____ _____
15. mis ____ _____
16. res ____ _____
17. ter ____ _____
18. ter ____ _____
19. vic ____ _____
20. won ____ _____

Column two

A.   bout
B.   cise
C.   derful
D.   emy
E.   ent
F.   erable
G.   fortable
H.   ful
I.   gree
J.   ligent
K.   low
L.   mous
M.   pendent
N.   prove
O.   rible
P.   rific
Q.   taurant
R.   ter
S.   tiful
T.   tory

© 1997 by The Center for Applied Research in Education

Advanced ESL

Name_____ Date_____

4-28 WE SMILED, TALKED, AND WAITED: THREE PRONUNCIATIONS OF *ED*

Final *ed* has a /t/ sound after voiceless consonants like /k/ or /f/. *Walked,* for example, is pronounced *walkt.* Final *ed* is pronounced /d/ after voiced consonants like /z/ or /v/. The *ed* in *sneezed,* for example, is pronounced /d/. Final *ed* is pronounced /d/ after /t/ and /d/. For example, *needed* is pronounced need /∂d/. Put the *ed* words below in the correct columns. *Be sure to copy the circled letters correctly.* If your answers are correct, the circled letters, *in order,* will spell a popular proverb. Can you explain it? Use the back of this sheet for your answer.

/∂/

1. ⓦalked
2. ⓡained
3. ⓟounded
4. shⓐved
5. fⓞlded
6. watⓒhed
7. coⓤnted
8. soⓡted
9. talkⓔd
10. fⓘnished
11. kⓘlled
12. enⓙoyed
13. ⓢnowed
14. viⓢited
15. kⓘssed
16. explaⓘned
17. ⓣouched
18. wanⓣed

/t/	/d/	/∂d/
ⓦalked		

© 1997 by The Center for Applied Research in Education

4-29 WHO'LL BE AT THE PARTY?:
QUESTION WORDS CONTRACTED WITH VERBS

In spoken English, *am, is, are, will, did, have, has, would,* and sometimes *had* are contracted with question words like *what, who, when, where,* and *how.* Your teacher will mix up the order of the sentences below and read them, pronouncing the contracted forms as Americans usually do. You will write the words you hear *uncontracted.* For example, if you hear, "When-uhl he come?" you'll write, "When will." If you hear, "Wherez my book?" you'll write, "Where is." If you hear, "Who-uv you seen?" you'll write, "Who have." Write your answers on the back of this sheet.

1. Where'm I supposed to be at 10:00?
2. Why's she crying?
3. When's he coming?
4. Where're they going?
5. Why're they shouting?
6. How're they getting along?
7. When'll you be back?
8. Who'll be there?
9. What'll you buy?
10. Where'd he go?
11. What'd he see?
12. How'd he like New York?
13. Why's he gone?
14. Where's he been?
15. What's he bought?
16. What's he eating?
17. When's he coming?
18. How's he feeling?
19. How'd he get to New York?
20. How'd you like some soda?
21. What've you eaten?
22. Where've they gone?
23. Where've you been?
24. How've you been?
25. Who've you seen lately?

These kids'll be at
the party.

© 1997 by The Center for Applied Research in Education

Advanced ESL

SECTION FIVE

SOCIAL PHRASES

5-1   HI, I'M ROSA: MAKING FRIENDS

Following the pattern, write a conversation under each of the pictures below.

Pattern

A. "Hi, I'm *Rosa*. What's your name?"
B. "Hi, Rosa. I'm *Krystyna*."
A. "Nice to meet you, *Krystyna*.
   Where are you from?"
B. "I'm from *Warsaw*. How about you?"
A. "I'm from *Mexico City*. How do you
   like America?"
B. "*I like it fine.* How about you?"
A. "Me, too."

Rosa   Krystyna

© 1997 by The Center for Applied Research in Education

1.

Toshi,   Gregor,

Tokyo   Moscow

            "I think it's
            great."

A._____
B._____
A._____
B._____
A._____
B._____
A._____

2.

Zoa,   Ho Buom,

Nigeria   Korea

            "I like it, but
            I think English
            is hard."

A._____
B._____
A._____
B._____
A._____
B._____
A._____

5-1 Hi, I'm Rosa: Making Friends *(Continued)*

A. _____

B. _____

A. _____

B. _____

A. _____

B. _____

A. _____

© 1997 by The Center for Applied Research in Education

3.

Hans,
Berlin

Yoko,
Osaka

"America's okay,
but I'm homesick."

5-2 HOW ARE YOU DOING?: ASSORTED ANSWERS

Sometimes Americans say, "How are you doing?" or "How are things going?" instead of "How are you?" Do you know how to answer this friendly question? To test yourself, blacken the boxes of the correct answers in the grid. If your choices are correct, you will form another popular greeting.

1	2	3	4	5	6	7
8	9	10	11	12	12	14
15	16	17	18	19	20	21

1. "The fine."
2. "Fine."
3. "Am great."
4. "Great."
5. "Hot."
6. "Not so hot."
7. "Am swell."
8. "So and so."
9. "Swell."
10. "Terrific."
11. "Wonderful."
12. "Most terrific."
13. "So so."
14. "Not hot."
15. "I am terrible."
16. "I'm fine."
17. "Right."
18. "Lousy."
19. "I am a lousy person."
20. "O.K."
21. "Not so O.K."

"How are you doing?"

© 1997 by The Center for Applied Research in Education

5-3   HOW ABOUT A SODA?: MAKING SUGGESTIONS

Study the pattern. Then write the three suggestion forms under each picture. Some are done for you.

Pattern

What shall we have? (Sometimes *have* is used to mean *eat* or *drink*.)

1. Why don't we have a soda?
2. How about a soda?
3. Let's have a soda.

A.   What shall we do?

1. Why don't we go skating?
2. _____ going _____?
3. _____.

B.   What shall we eat?

1. _____?
2. _____?
3. _____.

C.   Who shall we ask to the party?

1. _____?
2. _____?
3. _____.

Cora and Dora

© 1997 by The Center for Applied Research in Education

Name_____   Date_____

5-3   HOW ABOUT A SODA? *(CONTINUED)*

D.   Where shall we go?

    1. Why don't we go to the zoo?

    2. _____ going to the _____ ?

    3. _____.

E.   What kind of book shall we buy?

    1. Why don't we buy a western?

    2. _____?

    3. _____.

A western

F.   What kind of pet shall we get?

    1. _____?

    2. _____?

    3. _____.

© 1997 by The Center for Applied Research in Education

Name _____ Date _____

5-4   HAPPY TALK: LOOKING FORWARD TO

Do you understand the expression, "Looking forward to"? Circle the letters beside events people look forward to. Then place these letters, *in order*, in the blanks below. If your choices are correct, you will spell an event that most people *don't* look forward to.

A   __ __ __ __ __ __   __ __ __ __ __ __ __ __ __

(A.) A vacation
G. A broken arm
H. A hard test
D. A date with someone you like
E. A delicious dinner
X. A tornado
Y. An automobile accident
N. A wedding
Q. A fire
R. A fall on the ice
S. Getting a bad cold
T. Christmas or Hanukkah
A. A party
J. A bad grade
K. An earthquake
L. Graduation
S. An airplane crash
A. A high grade
B. A toothache
C. An earache
P. Thanksgiving dinner
D. A backache
P. Going shopping
H. A shipwreck
J. A robbery
O. A visit from your best friend
G. Going to the hospital
C. Losing your wallet
I. Meeting interesting people
N. Going to Disneyland
B. Taking bad-tasting medicine

T. Getting rich
U. Having an operation
M. Buying a new car
U. Falling in a manhole
V. Cutting your toe
E. Going to Paris
B. Below-zero weather
C. A thunderstorm
N. The weekend
F. A friend getting mad at you
T. New Year's Eve

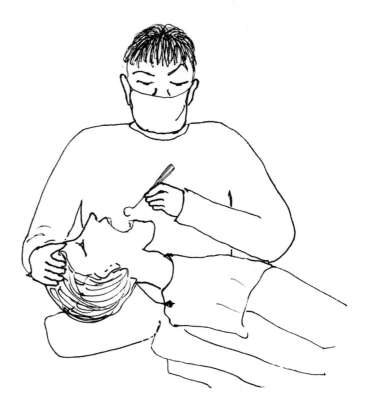

© 1997 by The Center for Applied Research in Education

Beginning ESL

Name_____   Date _____

5-5   OVER EASY: RESTAURANT TALK

Do you know how to order breakfast, a hot dog, or a steak dinner in a restaurant? Test yourself by circling the correct answers below. The letters beside the correct answers in each group will spell a word that tells you your choices are correct.

1. How do you want your eggs?

(C)   Over easy
(D)   Upside down
(I)   Hardly boiled
(O)   Hard boiled
(G)   Make me a scrambled
(R)   Scrambled
(A)   Easy over
(R)   Poached
(B)   Easy up
(E)   Soft boiled
(N)   Smoached
(C)   Sunnyside up
(F)   Make me a poached
(Y)   Full moon side up
(H)   Boiled soft
(T)   Make me an omelet

<u>C</u> __ __ __ __ __ __

3. How do you take your coffee?

(I)   Brown
(M)   The works
(O)   With cream and sugar
(P)   Creamy
(J)   Sweet
(K)   Black
(L)   Over easy
(M)   Down easy

__ __

4. What do you want on your hot dog?

(Y)   The works
(G)   Don't give me the works
(W)   Boiled onions
(T)   Hold the works
(E)   Catsup and mustard, hold the onions and relish
(F)   Catsup with mustard, keep the onions and relish
(R)   Mustard, don't hold the relish and catsup
(S)   Onions and relish, hold the catsup and mustard

__ __ __

2. How do you want your steak?

(D)   Bloody rare
(C)   Low done
(O)   Well done
(F)   Half done
(L)   Rarely
(K)   Medium rare
(W)   Done good
(V)   Medium done well
(A)   Rare
(M)   Done well
(Y)   Blood rare

__ __ __ __

© 1997 by The Center for Applied Research in Education

5-6 How About You?: Assorted Meanings

There are many possible answers to the question, "How about you?" The meaning of the question depends upon the words that precede it. To show your understanding, match the questions and answers below. Place the letter before each answer next to the correct questions. Then transfer the letters to the numbered blanks below these directions. If your answers are correct, you will spell a popular English proverb. Can you explain it? Use the back of this sheet for your answer.

$$\overline{}_{6} \; \overline{}_{7} \; \overline{}_{7} \; \overline{}_{5} \qquad \overline{}_{2} \; \overline{}_{3} \; \overline{}_{4} \; \overline{}_{7} \; \overline{}_{9} \; \overline{}_{3} \qquad \overline{}_{11} \; \overline{}_{7} \; \overline{}_{10}$$

$$\overline{}_{6} \; \overline{}_{3} \; \overline{A}_{1} \; \overline{}_{8}.$$

Questions

1. I'm feeling blue today. How about you? __A__
2. Nothing interesting happens in my life. How about you? _____
3. My English teacher gives too much homework. How about yours? _____
4. I had a great weekend. How about you? _____
5. My parents won't let me come home after midnight. How about yours? _____
6. I studied half the night for that exam. How about you? _____
7. I didn't get a good grade. How about you? _____
8. I was tired after track. How about you? _____
9. I don't like reading poetry. How about you? _____
10. My car's always in the shop. How about yours? _____
11. I'm really having fun this semester. How about you? _____

Answers

A. I'm kind of sad, too.
B. I'm bored, too.
C. I'd love to go.
D. Next time.
E. He loads us down, too.
F. I did, too. I had a date with a terrific girl.
G. Never.
H. I went to Disneyland.
I. Whenever you want to.
J. I ate too much, too.
K. Mine say 1:00 A.M. is okay.
L. I did, too. I didn't get any sleep.
M. We went to Alaska.
N. In the afternoon.
O. I did lousy, too.
P. I'm beat, too.
Q. I'm sick, too.
R. All literature in English is hard.
S. We're going to McDonald's.
T. I met two new kids.
U. Mine always needs repairs, too.
V. I like cats, too.
W. I don't like pigeons either.
X. Let's go home.
Y. I'm having a great time, too.

© 1997 by The Center for Applied Research in Education

5-7   WHAT TO SAY WHEN:
ASSORTED SOCIAL PHRASES

Match social phrases and situations by placing the situation letters in the blanks beside the social phrases.

Social phrases

1. How are you? How are you doing? How are things going? __G__
2. So long. _____
3. Good luck. _____
4. Same to you. _____
5. You, too. _____
6. May I help you? _____
7. Congratulations! _____
8. See you later. _____
9. Pleasant dreams. _____
10. Tough luck! _____
11. Please forgive me. _____
12. Excuse me. I beg your pardon. _____
13. Have fun. Have a good time. _____
14. Watch out! _____
15. How do you do? Nice to meet you. _____
16. May I use your telephone. _____
17. I'm sorry I'm late. _____
18. Have a good day. _____
19. Have a good trip. _____
20. Are you okay? _____

Situations

A. It is afternoon. You will see your friend in the evening.
B. Your friend doesn't see a car coming.
C. Your friend looks sick. You are worried.
D. Your friend got a poor grade on the math test.
E. Words said to a customer by a salesperson.
F. Your friend is taking a vacation.
G. You meet a friend in the hall.
H. Your friend has been waiting for you for twenty minutes.
I. Your mom is leaving for work in the morning.
J. You accidentally push someone on the bus.
K. You are saying goodbye.
L. Someone says, "Happy holidays."
M. Your friend has a job interview.
N. You are being introduced to someone.
O. Your friend has been admitted to a good college.
P. Someone says, "Have a good weekend."
Q. Your mom is going to sleep.
R. You said something unkind to your friend.
S. You are in a friend's home. You need to call home.
T. Your friend is going to a dance.

© 1997 by The Center for Applied Research in Education

5-8   I LOVE YOUR SWEATER: CLOTHES COMPLIMENTS

Study the compliments below and complete the sentences under each picture.

Compliments

1. What a *cute* skirt you're wearing.
2. What a *cute* skirt you have on.
3. That's a *cute* skirt you're wearing.
4. That's a *cute* skirt you have on.
5. That skirt really looks *cute*.
   (*Also:* pretty, beautiful, attractive, gorgeous, stunning, fabulous)
6. I *love* your sweater. (*Also:* like)
7. That's a very *nice* sweater you're wearing.
   (*Also:* pretty, cute, attractive)

A.

Tuxedo, tux

What a handsome _____.

That tux really _____.

I _____.

B.

Yuko   Yoko

Yuko is trying on clothes in a fitting room. Yoko is watching. What are some things Yoko might say about the dress Yuko is trying on?

_____

_____

_____

© 1997 by The Center for Applied Research in Education

5-9   THAT'S VERY SWEET OF YOU: WORDS OF PRAISE

Complete each conversation with suitable words of praise. (There is more than one appropriate answer.)

1. That's very *sweet* of you.	(*Also:* nice, kind, generous,
2. How *sweet* of you.	thoughtful, considerate)
3. You're being very *sweet*.	
4. You're so *sweet*.	
5. What a *clever* idea.	(*Also:* good, great, terrific,
6. That's a *clever* idea.	wonderful, fabulous)

1. SLIM: Let's have a surprise party for Stacy in the park.

   YOKO: _____

2. TADEUSZ: Natasha is home with a cold. I'm going to bring her flowers.

   KRYSTYNA: _____

3. TOSHI: That elderly woman is carrying two heavy packages. I'm going to help her.

   ROSA: _____

4. SLIM: I want to buy you something for your birthday that you really want.

   STACY: _____

5. GEORGE: I have more sweaters than I need. I'm going to give some to the new kid who doesn't have a single sweater.

   GLORIA: _____

6. MURAD: I think we should decorate our ESL room with flags from everybody's countries.

   GRETCHEN: _____

7. NISME: Mr. and Mrs. Sikand have students from all over the world. I think we should get them that new seven-language dictionary.

   OLAF: _____

8. LI: My mother has bad backaches. I'm going to save money from my part-time job and buy her a vibrating chair.

   ZOA: _____

9. GREGOR: Let's tape our English classes and study the tapes every night.

   YOKO: _____

© 1997 by The Center for Applied Research in Education

5-10 MAY I CALL YOU TONIGHT?: REQUESTS AND PERMISSION

Study the patterns. Then put the letters beside the correct sentences in the blanks. If your choices are correct, you will spell a common American compliment. Would you say it in your native language?

$$\overline{}_{5} \quad \overline{}_{7}\ \overline{}_{8}\ \overline{}_{13}\ \overline{}_{3} \quad \overline{}_{14}\ \overline{}_{8}\ \overline{}_{12}\ \overline{}_{9} \quad \overline{}_{4}\ \overline{\underset{1}{A}}\ \overline{}_{11}.$$

Patterns

Requests: Would you help me? Could you help me? Will you help me? Can you help me?
Asking permission: May I use your pen?
NOTE: "May" gives permission. "Can" relates to ability.

---

1. (A) Would you help me with my homework?
2. (D) May you help me?
3. (E) May I use your telephone?
4. (H) May I look at your notes?
5. (I) Can you open the window?
6. (C) Can you borrow my pencil?
7. (L) May I use your dictionary?
8. (O) Could you listen to my speech?
9. (R) May I go to a movie tonight?
10. (D) Would I borrow your pen?
11. (T) May I use the car tonight?
12. (U) Will you walk to the store with me?
13. (V) Would you let me work for you after school?
14. (Y) May I visit you tonight?
15. (F) Will I use your pencil?

© 1997 by The Center for Applied Research in Education

5-11   I'm Sorry, I Didn't Catch That: Asking People to Repeat

First, study the different ways of asking people to repeat something you didn't understand. Then fill in the blanks in the sentences that follow.

Ways of asking people to repeat what they've said:

1. *I'm sorry.* Could you repeat that? (*Also:* Excuse me, Pardon me, I beg your pardon)
2. I'm sorry. *Could* you say that again more slowly? (*Also:* Can you, Will you, Would you)
3. I'm sorry. I didn't *catch* what you said. (*Also:* hear, understand, quite understand, follow, get)
4. I beg your pardon.
5. I'm sorry. What did you say?
6. I'm sorry. What was that?
7. I'm sorry. I didn't *follow* you. (*Also:* understand, hear, get)
8. I'm sorry. I don't understand.
9. I'm sorry. I didn't catch that.

---

1. "Howwuzthemovelastnight?"
   I'm sorry. Could _____ you repeat that _____?

2. "When'er yougoinhome tovisityourfolks?"
   I'm _____. I _____ get _____ you said.

3. "Do yu think the math test'l behard?"
   _____. Will you say _____?

4. "TheBullswonthe game!"
   I _____.

5. "Some kidz don'tstudythe waytheyought to."
   I'm sorry. _____?

6. "Whatsthepopulationof China?"
   I beg your pardon. _____ catch _____.

7. "Theteachersaid allhallpasses hafta besigned."
   Excuse me. I didn't _____ understand _____.

8. "Please read chapter 81, pages 224 to 242."
   I beg your pardon. I _____ follow _____.

9. "You don't have to answer study questions 7 through 11 on page 211."
   I'm sorry. _____ understand.

10. "Wow! Slimmadeanother basket."
    I'm sorry. What _____?

© 1997 by The Center for Applied Research in Education

5-12 DOING ANYTHING SATURDAY NIGHT?: PLANNING A DATE

Here are some social phrases that can be used in planning an evening out. However, the phrases are not in correct order. Place phrase numbers in the blanks under the pictures to show conversational sequence and the person speaking.

1.

Maria   *Pedro*

___ ___ ___ ___ ___ ___

1. "Why, no, I'm not."
2. "Sounds great."
3. "I'd love 'em both."
4. "Hi, Maria. I was wondering if you're doing anything Saturday night."
5. "I'll pick you up about 7:00. Does that sound okay?"
6. "How about pizza and a movie?"

2.

Stacy   *Slim*

___ ___ ___ ___ ___ ___

1. "I really don't think so. I really just want to stay home tonight and watch TV."
2. "Hi, Stacy. I'm calling to see if you'd like to go dancing tonight."
3. "I don't think so. I'm not really in the mood for a movie."
4. "Thanks for calling, but I just don't feel like dancing."
5. "How about just going to a movie?"
6. "Well, is there anything you'd like to do?"

3.

Toshi   *Yoko*

___ ___ ___ ___ ___ ___

1. "In an hour. That'll be great."
2. "Would your folks mind if we played CD's?"
3. "Hi, Yoko. I was wondering if I could drop by tonight."
4. "Okay. I'll be over in about an hour."
5. "That would be swell. I'd love to see you tonight."
6. "No, I don't think they'd mind at all."

© 1997 by The Center for Applied Research in Education

5-13   MAY I SHOW YOU A LOVELY PURPLE AND ORANGE DRESS?: SHOPPING

Study the pattern, and then complete the conversations below each picture. Explain in your own words why you don't want what the salesperson is suggesting.

<table>
<tr><td>

Pattern

A. "May I help you?"
B. "Yes, I'm looking for *a heavy winter coat.*"
A. "I'm sorry, it's spring now. May I show you a stunning spring coat?"
B. "No, thank you. It's cold out, and I don't want a spring coat."

</td></tr>
</table>

Heavy winter coat

© 1997 by The Center for Applied Research in Education

1.

One-piece swim suit

A. "May I help you?"

B. _____

A. "I'm sorry. Bikinis are in style this year. May I show you a darling bikini?"

B. _____
_____
_____

2.

Simple black dress

A. "May I help you?"

B. _____

A. "I'm sorry, everyone is wearing purple and orange dresses this year. May I show you a lovely purple and orange dress?"

B. _____
_____
_____

© 1997 by The Center for Applied Research in Education

3.

Raincoat

A. "May I help you?"

B. _____

A. "I'm sorry. We don't have any raincoats. This has been a dry season. May I show you a handsome overcoat?"

B. _____
_____
_____

4.

Knee-length skirt

A. "May I help you?"

B. _____

A. "I'm sorry. Everyone is wearing mini-skirts this year. May I show you an adorable mini-skirt?"

B. _____
_____
_____

5.

Pair of comfortable
low-heeled shoes

A. "May I help you?"

B. _____

A. "I'm sorry. Low-heeled shoes aren't in style. May I show you a gorgeous pair of shoes with four-inch heels?"

B. _____
_____
_____

5-14   CAN YOU EVER FORGIVE ME?: APOLOGIES

Do you know how to apologize? Test yourself by choosing the correctly worded apology for each situation described below. Then transfer the circled letters in the *correct* apologies to the blank spaces in the words under these directions. The first one is done for you. If your choices are correct, you will complete four words that contain two letters referring to an important person: **ME.**

M E ___ ___   ___ ___ M E   M E ___ ___ ___
    I   2   3   4   5   6   7

___ M E ___ ___ ___ ___
 8   9   10   11   12

1. You accidentally push someone and say, "I'm very sorry." "I so sorry."

2. You step on someone's foot and say, "Too bad." "I'm terribly sorry."

3. You break a cup in someone's home and say, "Oh, how clumsy of me." "I'm really sad."

4. You tell someone he cheated you, then learn you were wrong. You say, "I owe you an apology." "I owe you."

5. You spill coffee on the tablecloth and say, "I'm extremely sorry." "I made a mistake."

6. You do something unkind to your friend and say, "I'd like to apologize." "I'd love to apologize."

7. You called when your friend was sleeping and say, "Leave me alone." "I'm awfully sorry."

8. You are whispering to a friend in class. The teacher is angry. You say, "I sorry." "I am sorry."

9. You forgot your girlfriend's birthday and say, "Please forgive me." "I'm terrible sorry."

10. Your friend lends you her favorite ring. You lose it and say, "Can you ever forgive me?" "I'm very bad."

11. Your friend is meeting you for lunch. You are a half hour late and say, "I can't tell you how sorry I am." "I am wrong."

12. You make your friend angry and say, "I want to apologize." "I want to be sorry."

© 1997 by The Center for Applied Research in Education

ANSWER KEY

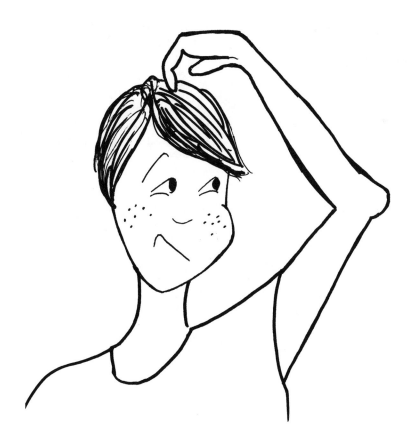

1-1 Give Me a Hand: Body Parts

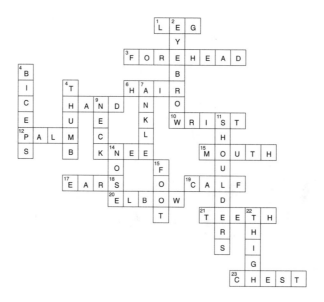

1-2 Appearances Count: Clothing Words

Answers can be given in any order.

1. A. Tie
   B. Cap
   C. Pair of pants
2. A. Shorts
   B. T-shirt
   C. Dress shirt
   D. Tank top
   E. Sweatpants
   F. Jeans
   G. Jacket
   H. Vest
   I. Gloves
   J. Socks
   K. Shoes
   L. Suit jacket
3. A. T-shirt
   B. Shorts
   C. Shoes

4. A. Shorts
   B. Pants
   C. Socks
   D. Shoes
   E. Gloves
5. A. Two sweaters
   B. A hat

6. A. Jacket
   B. Scarf
   C. Mittens
   D. High-heeled shoes

7. A. Dress

8. A. Boots
   B. Blouse
   C. Jackets
   D. Dress
   E. Suit

9. A. Sunglasses
   B. Skirt

10. A. Shoes
    B. Boots
    C. Mittens
    D. Sunglasses

BONUS QUESTION: "Appearances count" means that how a person looks is important. Nice clothes, cleanliness, and combed hair are important.

1-3 How's the Weather?: Weather Words

1. Winter
    Cold
    Freezing
    Frigid
    Icy

2. Fall or Autumn
    Breezy
    Chilly
    Clear
    Cool
    Dry
    Windy

3. Summer
    Hot
    Calm
    Clear
    Dry
    Sunny

4. Spring
    Calm
    Clear
    Mild
    Dry
    Warm

1-4 World of Nature: Birds and Bees

1. Horse
2. Insect
3. Porcupine
4. Pig
5. Ostrich
6. Parrot
7. Owl
8. Tiger
9. Anteater
10. Monkey
11. Unicorn
12. Squirrel

The first letters spell HIPPOPOTAMUS.

1-5 Yum, Yum: Food and Drink

Scrambled Words

1. COFFEE
2. COKE
3. CREAM
4. CHEESE
5. TUNA

6. SALMON
7. BANANA
8. KIWI
9. BREAD
10. CORNMEAL

11. BEEF
12. PORK
13. DUCK
14. SALT
15. MUSTARD

16. CRAB
17. SHRIMP
18. CARROTS
19. PEAS
20. CORN

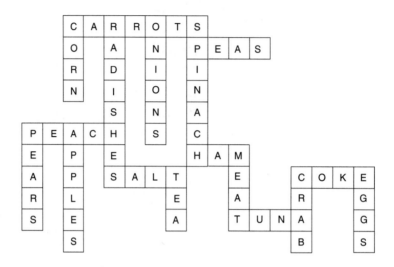

1-6 Pardon Me, Do You Have the Time?: Telling Time

1. W
2. A   PALINDROME: Was it a rat I saw.
3. S
4. I
5. T
6. A
7. R
8. A
9. T
10. I
11. S
12. A
13. W

1-7 Shape Up: Shapes and Lines

A. 23
B. 12
C. 21
D. 15
E. 16
F. 10
G. 13
H. 11
I. 18
J. 22
K. 7
L. 4
M. 3
N. 9
O. 1
P. 8
Q. 24
R. 14
S. 19
T. 17
U. 2
V. 20

Unshaded numbers (5 and 6) form a hexagon.

1-8 Day Before Yesterday: Time Expressions

2.   The day before yesterday was Tuesday the 9th.

3.   Tomorrow is Thursday the 12th.

4.   The day after tomorrow is Friday the 13th.

6.   Wednesday after next is the 25th.

7.   Last Wednesday was the 4th.

9.   Last month was December.

10.   The month before last was November.

11.   Next month is February.

13-23. Answers will vary.

1-9 He's Worth a Million Bucks: Money Words

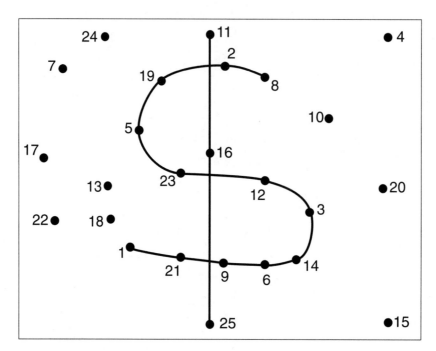

A. 11
B. 16
C. 25
D. 8
E. 2
F. 19
G. 5
H. 23
I. 12
J. 3
K. 14
L. 6
M. 9
N. 21
O. 1

1-10 Bingo: Sports and Recreations

			T	R	A	C	K
	T	E	N	N	I	S	
		C	A	R	D	S	
S	W	I	M	M	I	N	G
	D	I	V	I	N	G	
	B	I	N	G	O		

1-11　Silver Blades: Sports and Recreations

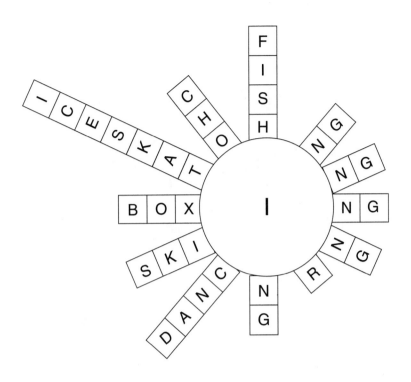

1-12　It's a Homer: Sports and Recreations

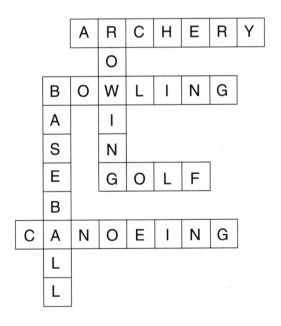

1-13 Word Search: More Sports and Recreations

M	A	N	H	O	M	E	R	U	N	G	O	L
M	E	T	O	B	O	G	G	A	N	I	N	G
H	E	S	C	F	O	O	T	B	A	L	L	I
B	A	S	K	E	T	B	A	L	L	Y	O	U
H	I	U	E	Y	C	A	N	O	E	I	N	G
I	T	R	Y	O	D	A	R	C	H	E	R	Y
N	O	F	Y	E	S	I	R	I	D	I	N	G
O	H	I	C	A	R	D	V	J	A	Z	Z	O
U	S	N	T	R	A	C	K	I	B	A	L	L
U	P	G	B	O	X	I	N	G	N	O	F	F
W	A	T	E	R	S	K	I	I	N	G	O	X

1-14   No Left Turn: Road Signs

A. 17
B. 19
C. 8
D. 9
E. 1
F. 7
G. 2
H. 15
I. 4
J. 13
K. 5
L. 12
M. 18
N. 6
O. 16
P. 3
Q. 11
R. 10
S. 14

Vocabulary Review

1. A
2. A
3. C
4. C
5. B
6. B
7. B
8. A
9. B
10. C

6. Sixth, 6th
7. Seventh, 7th
8. Eighth, 8th
9. Ninth, 9th
10. Tenth, 10th
11. Eleventh, 11th
20. Twentieth, 20th
21. Twenty-first, 21st
22. Twenty-second, 22nd
23. Twenty-third, 23rd
30. Thirtieth, 30th
32. Thirty-first, 31st

16. Sixteen
17. Seventeen
21. Twenty-one
22. Twenty-two
23. Twenty-three
31. Thirty-one
32. Thirty-two
41. Forty-one
47. Forty-seven
51. Fifty-one
52. Fifty-two
65. Sixty-five
78. Seventy-eight
86. Eighty-six
99. Ninety-nine
109. One hundred nine
119. One hundred nineteen
155. One hundred fifty-five

1-16 The Butcher, the Baker, the Candlestick Maker: Jobs and Professions

1. 4, B
2. 6, C
3. 2, A
4. 1, D
5. 3, F
6. 5, E

1-17   Yes, Your Honor: More Jobs and Professions

1.   3, B
2.   4, C
3.   1, E
4.   5, A
5.   2, D

1-18   Leaky Pipe: Still More Jobs and Professions

1.   4, A
2.   5, C
3.   1, B
4.   2, E
5.   3, D

1-19   Moon Walk: More Career Choices

1.   4, A
2.   5, B
3.   3, E
4.   2, D
5.   1, C

1-20   All in the Family: Family Words

1.   P
2.   B
3.   R
4.   G
5.   J
6.   K
7.   M
8.   Q
9.   A
10.   I
11.   H
12.   C
13.   F
14.   D
15.   O
16.   N
17.   S
18.   L
19.   E

1-21   Map Rap: Geography Words

1. 12,   A
2. 4,   N
3. 7,   T
4. 1,   A
5. 17,   R
6. 25,   C
7. 21,   T
8. 14,   I
9. 19,   C
10. 10, A

1-22   Double Trouble: Homonyms

1.   1   C
2.   9   A
3.   5   R
4.   7   N
5.   8   A
6.   2   T
7.   3   I
8.   6   O
9.   4   N

BONUS QUESTION: To bore is to drill a hole and to cause to lose interest.

1-23   My Aching Head: More Homonyms

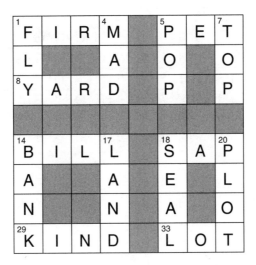

1-24 Slim Ate Eight Hamburgers: Homophones

Incorrect
5
10
12
17

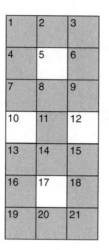

1-25 Another Way of Saying This: Synonyms

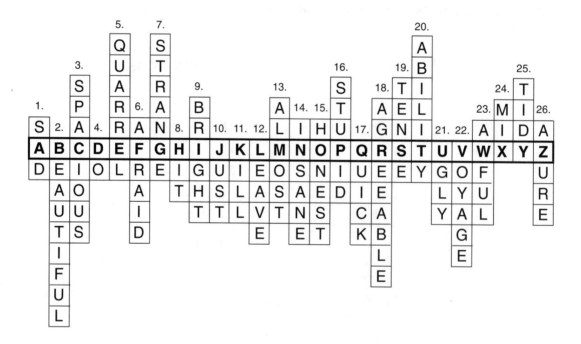

1-26 You Got Me Wrong: Antonyms

1.	W	I	C	K	E	D

1. W I C K E D
2. L O U D
3. N E V E R
4. O D D
5. T E N D E R
6. S M A R T
7. F A T
8. F U L L
9. L O V E L Y

10. T A M E
11. S W E E T
12. O F T E N
13. C R U E L
14. L A Z Y

1-27 Things Aren't What They Seem: Idiom Literalized

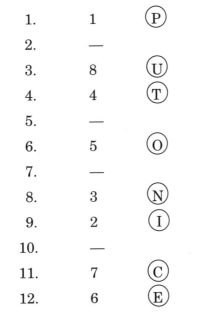

1.   1   (P)
2.   —
3.   8   (U)
4.   4   (T)
5.   —
6.   5   (O)
7.   —
8.   3   (N)
9.   2   (I)
10. —
11. 7   (C)
12. 6   (E)

Circled letters spell: Put on ice

1-28   What Did you Say?: Idiom and Meaning

1. M
2. O
3. N
4. E
5. Y
6. T
7. A
8. L
9. K
10. S
11. F
12. I
13. S
14. H
15. Y
16. C
17. B
18. J
19. G
20. D
21. Q
22. Z
23. P
24. V
25. X
26. W
27. R
28. U

Numbers 1-15 spell two idiomatic expressions: Money Talks, Fishy

BONUS QUESTION: *Money talks* means that money is important and helpful. Money impresses people. When something is *fishy,* it is suspicious.

1-29   A Yellow Blueblood: Color Idiom

Wording of answers will vary.

1.   A bruised Caucasian

2.   An intelligent factory worker

3.   A sad office worker

4.   A cowardly aristocrat

5.   I owe money infrequently.

6.   I was out of debt unexpectedly.

7.   I was embarrassed because I was frightened.

8.   He avoided work because he wasn't feeling well.

1-30 It's a Piece of Cake: Partitives

1. F
2. I
3. N
4. H
5. O
6. C
7. P
8. K
9. A
10. L
11. S
12. E
13. T

First idiom: A piece of cake
Second idiom: A flash in the pan

1-31 Blind as a Bat: Animal Idioms

	A 1	B 4	
C 11	D 6	E 7	F 2
G 8	H 10	I 3	J 5
	K 9	L 12	

A.	Blind as a bat	1
B.	Busy as a bee	4
C.	Scaredy cat	11
D.	Dumb as a dodo	6
E.	Sly as a fox	7
F.	Big as a horse	2
G.	Brave as a lion	8
H.	Is he a man or a mouse	10
I.	Stubborn as a mule	3
J.	Slow as a turtle	5
K.	Wise as an owl	9
L.	Dirty as a pig	12

1-32   Don't Put Your Foot in Your Mouth: Put Family

A.   4
Accept a fixed idea that's strange or even slightly crazy.

B.   6
Give someone a hint or idea that will cause him or her to act.

C.   5
Put all one's efforts, interests, and hopes into a single plan.

D.   3
Express one's opinion.

E.   1
Speak carelessly or rudely, embarrassing oneself or others.

F.   7
Make someone angry or jealous.

G.   2
Work hard, make an effort.

H.   8
Think about problems with another person.

1-33   Don't Pull My Leg: Body Idiom

A.   2
B.   3
C.   4
D.   1
E.   5
F.   6

1-34   It Smells Fishy: Fish Idiom

1.   T   A person without feelings
2.   H   The most important person in a group
3.   E   Someone who is important only in a small group
4.   L   Not belonging to any group or category
5.   E   Many other people suited for a job
6.   T   Take too much alcohol
7.   T   Suggest that other people say nice things about you
8.   E   Have other things to do
9.   R   A confusing affair
10. I   Drown in a river, lake, or ocean

The answer to the riddle, "What part of Mexico is in Iraq?" is THE LETTER *I*.

BONUS QUESTION: Something appears strange or suspicious

1-35 As I Always Say: Everyday Idioms

1.	B	14.	R
2.	G	15.	Y
3.	I	16.	K
4.	D	17.	Q
5.	L	18.	W
6.	N	19.	V
7.	X	20.	S
8.	M	21.	U
9.	H	22.	P
10.	O	23.	E
11.	F	24.	T
12.	A	25.	C
13.	J		

1-36 Fit as a Fiddle: Common Comparisons

1. Rock
2. Ice
3. Fiddle
4. Glove
5. Peacock
6. Rail
7. Picture
8. Hills
9. Gold
10. Feather
11. House
12. Doornail
13. Pie
14. Thieves
15. Bird
16. Honey

1-37 *Break* Down the Door

1. Break down
2. Break in
3. Break out
4. Break up
5. Break out

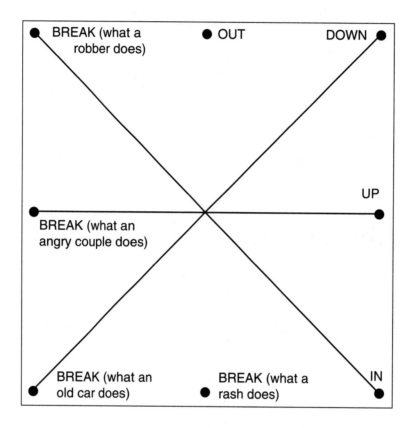

BONUS QUESTION: "To break into song" means to begin suddenly to speak or perform.

1-38 *Come* in Please

1. P(in)   Won't you *come in,* please.
2. M(oon)   *Come on.* I'm in a hurry.
3. C(over)   *Come over* to my house sometime.
4. P(up)   *Come up* the stairs carefully.
5. (To)oth   Why don't you *come to* a movie with me?

1-39 Don't *Do* Me In

1. H
2. O
3. L
4. D

5. H
6. I
7. S

8. N
9. O
10. S
11. E

If students' English is adequate, explain the difference between *smell* as a linking and non-linking verb.

1-40 Don't *Get* In Trouble

¹A	B	²O	U	³T					
C		N		⁴H	U	R	⁵T		
R				R		⁶O	N		
⁷O	U	T		O					
S				⁸U	P		⁹I	¹⁰N	
S		¹¹B	I	G				E	
		A		¹³H	¹⁴U	N	G	R	Y
¹⁵B	A	C	K		P			V	
A		K						O	
C			¹⁷I		¹⁸O	N		¹⁹U	P
K		²⁰A	T		N			S	

1-41 I'd Like to Take Her Out: Separable Verbs

1. on, on, on
2. up, up, up
3. up, up, up
4. off, off, off
5. out, out, out
6. on, on, on

1-42   The Robber Got In: Non-Separable Verbs

2.   The robber got into the empty house.
3.   Ranjana and Ashoke got off the plane from Bombay.
4.   Tadeusz got on the bus to Minneapolis.
5.   Maria had a cold, but she got over it.
6.   Nisme looked for her ESL book, but she couldn't find it.
7.   Pedro ran into his friend in the hall.

1-43   I Want to Travel, But I Can't Stand Flying: Verbs with Infinitives & Gerunds

Answers will vary, but should use infinitives and gerunds correctly.

1-44   Pop the Question: Boy and Girl Talk

A.   20
B.   15
C.   3
D.   22
E.   1
F.   17
G.   21
H.   11
I.   12
J.   19
K.   4
L.   8
M.   7
N.   5
O.   13
P.   6
Q.   9
R.   14
S.   16
T.   10
U.   2
V.   18
W.   23
X.   24
Y.   25

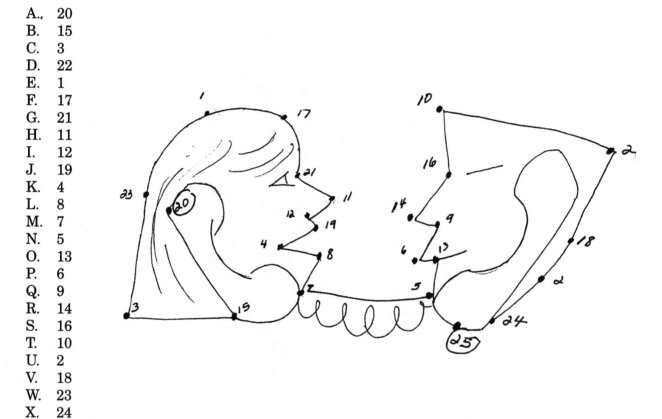

1-45   Potpourri: Miscellaneous Slang

A. 20
B. 6
C. 7
D. 17
E. 9
F. 15
G. 14
H. 12
I. 13
J. 11
K. 10
L. 16
M. 8
N. 18
O. 19
P. 5

A 20	B 6	C 7	D 17
E 9	F 15	G 14	H 12
I 13	J 11	K 10	L 16
M 8	N 18	O 19	P 5

1-46   Stone Soup: More Miscellaneous Slang

1. H
2. L
3. S
4. N
5. O
6. P
7. R
8. M
9. D
10. Q
11. B
12. C
13. A
14. I
15. J
16. K
17. E
18. F
19. T
20. U

1-47   Besides, I Want to Sit Beside You

Correct sentences

B
E
I
K

The answer to the riddle is BIKE.

1-48   Sometimes They Think They're in Love: Sometimes, Sometime

1. Sometimes
2. Sometimes
3. sometimes
4. sometimes
5. sometime
6. sometimes
7. sometime
8. sometimes
9. Sometimes
10. sometime
11. sometime
12. Sometimes
13. Sometimes
14. sometime
15. Sometimes
16. sometimes
17. sometimes

2-1   What's Its Name: Nouns

Arms
Blackboard
Blotter
Bookcase
Books
Boys
Bulletin Board
Chalk
Chin
Classroom
Desks
Door
Doorknob
Elbows
Eraser
Eyes
Floor
Geography
Girls
Glasses
Globe
Hair
Hands
Heads
Jacket
Man
Map
Mouth
Neck
Nose
Numbers
Paper
Pockets
Pointer
School

Seats
Shirts
Teacher
Thumbtacks
Tie
Walls
Windows

2-2 Of Mice and Men: Noun Plurals

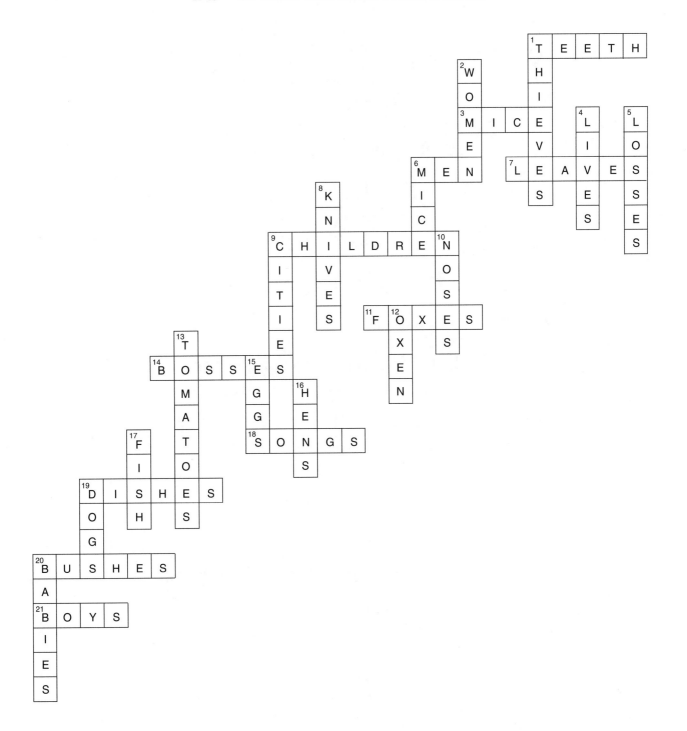

2-3 My Boss's Wife: Possessive Nouns

1. Natasha's parachute
2. Baby's tooth
3. Babies' teeth
4. Gorilla's ice cream cone
5. Skaters' sweaters

2-4 Run, Dick, Run: Basic Verbs

1. D
2. E
3. A
4. F
5. C
6. B
7. G
8. H

2-5 Hop, Skip, Jump: More Basic Verbs

1. D
2. H
3. E
4. B
5. G
6. A
7. C
8. F

2-6 Everybody Sing: Still More Basic Verbs

1. F
2. H
3. B
4. A
5. G
6. C
7. D
8. E

2-7 Slim Is Slim: Basic Adjectives

1. Cute   Skinny
   Little   Slim
   Pretty   Tall
   Short   Thin

2. Big
   Husky
   Muscular
   Strong

3. Angry
   Big
   Fierce
   Frightening
   Strong

4. Cheerful
   Happy
   Same

5. Itchy
   Sick
   Uncomfortable

6. Scared
   Frightened

2-8 Fat Cat: Adjective-Noun Review

1. Rock clock
2. Third bird
3. Fox box
4. Funny bunny
5. Vanilla gorilla
6. Ice mice
7. Bat hat

2-9 Thick Stick: Additional Noun-Adjective Review

1. Door floor
2. Bright light
3. Night fight
4. Mouse house
5. Flat hat
6. Cute flute

2-10 Very Well Done: Descriptive Adverbs

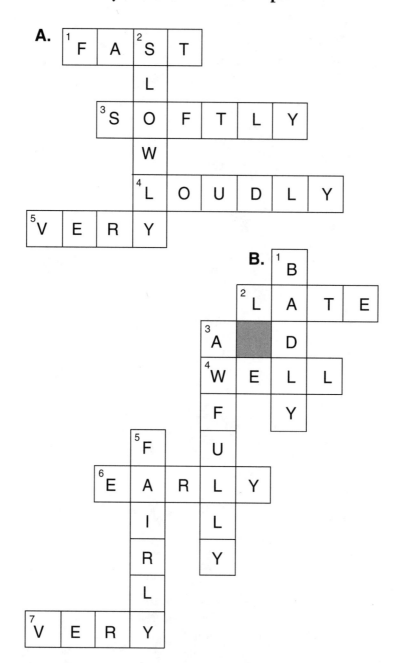

2-11 Slim Sometimes Studies: Frequency Adverbs

Answers will vary. Here are possible answers:

1. I *always* walk to school.
2. I *usually* eat eggs for breakfast.
3. I *often* eat hamburgers for lunch.
4. I *sometimes* drink cola.
5. I *rarely* play baseball.
6. I *never* fly to school.

2-12 Out of the Frying Pan and Into the Fire: Basic Prepositions

1. in
2. behind
3. above
4. in front of (**or** at **or** beside)
5. between
6. about
7. beside
8. at

2-13 On and Off: More Basic Prepositions

1. on
2. out of
3. against
4. off
5. with
6. through
7. under
8. over

2-14 This and That: Demonstrative Pronouns

1	2	3	4	5
6	7	8	9	10
11	12	13	14	15
16	17	18	19	20

2-15 You and Me: Personal Pronouns

A	P	A	U	N	O	M	A	A	A	S	A	H	N	A	A
1 P	2 E	3 R	4 S	5 O	6 N	7 A	8 L	9 P	10 R	11 O	12 N	13 O	14 U	15 N	16 S
E	N	E	E	R	E	N	L	E	T	N	D	T	T	T	K

2-16   A Boy, an Egg, and the Man in the Moon: Articles

1. An ape
2. A bee
3. An egg
4. A hamburger
5. An Indian (*or* A Native American)
6. A judge
7. An owl
8. A queen (*or* The Queen)

2-17   A, An, The: More Articles

1. An umbrella
2. A vine
3. A wig
4. An X-ray
5. A zipper
6. The Earth
7. The Sun
8. The Man in the Moon

2-18   How Many Words Are There in Grandmother?: Parts-of-Speech Review

Students will probably find many words not listed.

Nouns	*Verbs*	*Adjectives*	*Names*
Art	Am	Dear	Dan
Dart	Are	Grand	Don
Den	Ate	Great	Dot
Dog	Dent	Hot	Ed
Dot	Do	Mad	Meg
Garden	Done	Other	Ned
Garter	Eat	Red	Ron
Gem	Eaten	Tan	Tod
Gender	Get	Tom	
God	Go		
Hag	Gone	*Pronouns*	
Ham	Got	He	
Hand	Hat	Her	
Hat	Hate	Me	
Head	Met	Them	
Hem	Nod		
Hen	Ran	*Prepositions*	
Herd	Rate	At	
Hog	Read	On	
Man	Rot	To	
Men	Tag		
Moth	Tear	*Conjunctions*	
Mother	Tore	And	
Name	Torn	Nor	
Oar		Or	
Oat			
Rag		*Articles*	
Ram		A	
Rat		An	
Red		The	
Rod			
Tam		*Negatives*	
Tea		No	
Ten		Not	

2-19 I'm a Good Egg: Subject and Verb Agreement—*Be*

A. 1   (is)
B. 4   (are)
C. 9   (am)
D. 12   (is)
E. 13   (are)
F. 18   (are)
G. 20   (are)
H. 24   (are)
I. 26   (are)
J. 30   (is)
K. 33   (are)
L. 34   (are)
M. 39   (are)
N. 41   (are)
O. 45   (are)
P. 48   (are)
Q. 51   (is)
R. 53   (are)
S. 56   (am)
T. 59   (are)

2-20 To Be or Not to Be: Negative Agreement—*Be*

1. am not
2. aren't
3. isn't
4. aren't
5. aren't
6. aren't
7. aren't
8. aren't
9. isn't
10. aren't
11. aren't
12. am not
13. aren't
14. isn't
15. am not
16. isn't
17. aren't
18. aren't
19. isn't
20. aren't

2-21 Stacy Has a Guy: Subject and Verb Agreement—*Have*

Incorrect sentences
A
G
L

Missing word: GAL (Slang for *girl*)

2-22 The Money Tree: Some Indefinite Pronouns

1. D
2. E
3. G
4. M
5. N
6. O
7. R
8. S
9. T
10. W
11. Y

Proverb: Money doesn't grow on trees.
Meaning: It isn't easy to get money. Money is not readily available.
Rephrasing: Money grows on trees.
Meaning of rephrasing: Money is easy to get.

2-23 Space Savers: Pronoun Contractions

2. you're, you're
3. I'm
4. you're
5. It's
6. He's
7. It's, He's, he's, I'm, I'm
8. It's, You're
9. I'm, She's
10. They're
11. You're
12. I'm
13. You're, I'm, we're, I'm

2-24 Guys Like Gals: Subject and Verb Agreement—Action Verbs

1. R
2. V
3. O
4. T
5. V
6. Y
7. I
8. F
9. E
10. L
11. S

Decoded message: I love you
Method of code: First letters

2-25 To Have or Have Not: Negative Agreement—Action Verbs

1. don't like
2. doesn't eat
3. don't walk
4. doesn't love
5. don't speak
6. doesn't have
7. don't have
8. don't have
9. doesn't bark
10. don't have
11. doesn't dream
12. don't have
13. doesn't have
14. don't study
15. don't wear

2-26 Is Slim a Big Cheese?: Questions and Short Answers

2. Are Yuko and Yoko twins? Yes, they are.
3. Does Gregor bike to school? Yes, he does. Or: No, he doesn't.
4. Do George and Gloria like pizza? Yes, they do. Or: No, they don't.
5. Are you and I students? Yes, we are.
6. Do Toshi and Yoshi speak Japanese? Yes, they do.
7. Are you from Portugal? Yes, I am. Or: No, I'm not.
8. Do some kids drive to school? Yes, they do.
9. Does Slim have a ten-speed bike? Yes, he does.
10. Does Slim want a sports car? Yes, he does.
11. Do Slim and Tod have bikes? Yes, they do.
12. Does Maria need a new coat? Yes, she does. Or: No, she doesn't.
13. Do some girls wear too much lipstick? Yes, they do.
14. Are Slim and Tod big cheeses? Yes, they are. Or: No, they aren't.

2-27 Where Is Slim?: Question Words with *to Be*

2. D, G
3. A, D
4. H, F
5. I, J
6. C, B
7. B, C
8. F, E
9. G, I
10. J, H

2-28 When Does Class Start?: Question Words with Action Verbs

1. Where do his older brothers study?
2. Where do Mr. and Mrs. Sikand go every summer?
   When do Mr. and Mrs. Sikand go to India?
3. Why does he eat a lot of candy?
4. Where do they work?
   Because they like animals.
5. John gets up at 7 o'clock.

2-29 What Do You Think?: Who and What as Subject and Object

2
6

2-30 Quiz Kids Only: Review of Question Patterns

Incorrect sentences

4
6
1
3
8

Arithmetic problem

46 + 46 + 46 = 138

2-31 A Box of Chocolates and a Carton of Eggs: Subject and Verb Agreement—Intervening Phrases

1. E
2. G
3. H
4. I
5. N
6. S
7. T
8. U

Answer to problem: The sun is shining.

2-32 Will You, Won't You?: Future Tense—*Will*

1. will
2. won't or will not; I'll
3. you'll; I'll
4. I'll
5. He'll
6. will; we'll
7. you'll
8. won't or will not; won't or will not
9. will
10. They'll
11. they'll
12. you'll; will
13. won't
14. will; won't or will not

2-33 I'm Going to Be Your Girlfriend: Future Tense—*Be Going*

1. is going to be
2. is going to be
3. are not going to
4. am going to
5. are going to
6. are you going to eat
7. am going to eat
8. am going to eat
9. are you going to be
10. am
11. are going to
12. are
13. are you going to go to
14. am
15. am not going to be

2-34 What's He Doing?: Present Progressive, Yes/No, and Information Questions and Answers

L	Ⓘ	Ⓝ	Ⓖ	Y
P	E	Ⓞ	J	Q
X	R	Ⓦ	F	M

1. N
2. O
3. W
4. I
5. G

2-35 Stranger Than Fiction: Negative Forms of Present and Present Progressive

A. What is the automobile doing?
1. The automobile is flying.
2. The automobile isn't traveling on the ground in this picture.
3. Airplanes fly.
4. Automobiles don't fly.

B. What is the cat doing?
1. The cat is smoking a cigar.
2. A man isn't smoking a cigar in this picture.
3. Men smoke cigars.
4. Cats don't smoke cigars.

C. What is the octopus eating?
1. The octopus is eating a hamburger.
2. A person isn't eating a hamburger in this picture.
3. People eat hamburgers.
4. Octopuses don't eat hamburgers.

2-36   I Love You: Progressive and Non-Progressive Verbs

		P	A	Y		(18)
A	R	R	I	V	E	(10)
	H	O	P	E		(13)
		G	O			(3)
A	R	R	E	S	T	(5)
	F	E	E	D		(4)
		S	A	Y		(1)
	R	E	S	T		(9)
	B	R	I	N	G	(11)
	S	A	V	E		(16)
G	I	V	E			(19)

2-37   Either/Or: Verbs That Are Both Progressive and Non-Progressive

Correct answers

A
R
T
I
C
L
E
S

Mary likes words that begin with ARTICLES (*a, an, the*).

2-38   The Roast Is Smelling Good: More Verbs That Are Both Progressive and Non-Progressive

All the sentences are correct. The answer is zero. *Zero* is the last number in the equation. *Zero* times other numbers equals *zero*.

2-39 No Numbers in This One: Irregular Verbs

2-40 Hide and Seek: More Irregular Verbs

2. do, did, done
3. eat, ate, eaten
4. lend, lent, lent
5. go, went, gone
6. lie, lay, lain
7. lay, laid, laid
8. light, lit, lit
9. lose, lost, lost
10. read, read, read; *or* spread, spread, spread
11. ride, rode, ridden; *or* stride, strode, stridden
12. ring, rang, rung
13. rise, rose, risen
14. grow, grew, grown
15. set, set, set
16. take, took, taken
17. sweep, swept, swept; *or* weep, wept, wept; *or* take, took, taken
18. win, won, won; *or* wind, wound, wound
19. show, showed, shown
20. lead, led, led
21. put, put, put
22. rid, rid, rid
23. steal, stole, stolen
24. let, let, let
25. bet, bet, bet
26. dig, dug, dug
27. draw, drew, drawn
28. break, broke, broken

2-41 Add-Ons: More Practice with Irregular Verbs

Note: Students may think of others besides those given here.

2. find, found, found
3. eat, ate, eaten
4. weep, wept, wept
5. sing, sang, sung
6. shine, shined, shone; shined, shined
7. grow, grew, grown
8. bring, brought, brought; *or* wring, wrung, wrung
9. grind, ground, ground
10. spit, spat, spat
11. draw, drew, drawn
12. blow, blew, blown; *or* plow, plowed, plowed
13. kneel, knelt, knelt
14. hit, hit, hit; *or* sit, sat, sat
15. hit, hit, hit
16. forget, forgot, forgotten
17. send, sent, sent; *or* bend, bent, bent
18. hear, heard, heard
19. teach, taught, taught
20. bind, bound, bound
21. bend, bent, bent
22. fall, fell, fallen

2-42 Did You Ever See a Laughing Hyena?: Past Tense—*Ever, Never*

1. No, I never wore fancy duds.
2. No, I was never in the doghouse.
3. No, I never went on a blind date.
4. No, I was never in hot water.
5. No, I never had butterflies in my stomach.
6. No, I never played with fire.
7. No, I never met a bad egg.

2-43 Were You Out with a Cute Chick Last Night?: Past Tense Questions and Answers

1. Yes, I was out with a cute chick last night.
    No, I wasn't out with a cute chick last night.
2. Yes, Rosa let down her hair at Gregor's birthday party.
    No, Rosa didn't let down her hair at Gregor's birthday party.
3. Yes, Slim sold his car for chicken feed.
    No, Slim didn't sell his car for chicken feed.
4. Yes, Gregor lost his head over Natasha.
    No, Gregor didn't lose his head over Natasha.
5. Yes, George hit the books before the history test.
    No, George didn't hit the books before the history test.
6. Yes, I spread myself too thin during exam week.
    No, I didn't spread myself too thin during exam week.
7. Yes, I was out with a sour puss last night.
    No, I wasn't out with a sour puss last night.

2-44   Did You, Didn't You?: More Past Tense Questions and Answers

1. did; call
2. didn't
3. promised
4. promised; was
5. were
6. had
7. did; have
8. had
9. did; study
10. read
11. did; read
12. read
13. did; learn
14. learned; fought
15. didn't fight; made; didn't study; did; do; went
16. didn't go; went
17. broke
18. broke; didn't break
19. didn't; broken

2-45   I Saw a Laughing Hyena in My Yard Yesterday: Past and Present Perfect

1 I	2 D	3 E	4 A
5 D	6 E	7 A	8 N
9 E	10 A	11 S	12 T
13 A	14 N	15 T	16 S

2-46   I Haven't Seen You for Ages: Present Perfect—*For* or *Since*

Errors

1
3
4
6
8
9
11

There are seven errors. The answer to any arithmetic problem following the directions is seven.

2-47   Slim Had Spent All His Money: Past Perfect

1.   the cat had sat on the hat
2.   the prisoner had escaped
3.   left his house; begun to rain
4.   came running; had already stung the baby
5.   got to the game, Gregor had made a basket
6.   he had broken into a bakery and eaten fifteen pies

2-48   Where Was Martin When the Lights Went Out?: Past Progressive

1.   The monkey was hanging by his tail when he fell out of the tree.
     When the monkey fell out of the tree, he was hanging by his tail.

2.   Martin was standing in the dark when the lights went out.
     When the lights went out, Martin was standing in the dark.

3.   Big Hunk was playing ice hockey when he sprained his ankle.
     When he sprained his ankle, Big Hunk was playing ice hockey.

4.   Olaf was skiing when he got tangled up in a tree.
     When he got tangled up in a tree, Olaf was skiing.

5.   Masha was building a bookcase when she hit her finger with a hammer.
     When Masha was building a bookcase, she hit her finger with a hammer.

6.   Nerd was putting his foot in his mouth when he broke his tooth.
     When Nerd broke his tooth, he was putting his foot in his mouth.

2-49   What'll You Be Doing Tonight: Future Progressive

Answers will vary.

2-50   He'd Been Working All Day: Present and Past Perfect Progressive

1.   A
2.   C
3.   L
4.   M
5.   N
6.   P

Palindrome: A MAN, A PLAN, A CANAL, PANAMA

2-51 Three Ugly Monsters: Comparison of Adjectives—One Syllable, Three Syllables, *Y* Endings

A.   1.   is smaller than
        2.   is smaller than
        3.   is larger than
        4.   is more beautiful
        5.   is more beautiful
        6.   is more beautiful than
        7.   is the most beautiful

B.   Answers will vary.

2-52 The "Worstest" Pie: Irregularly Compared Adjectives, Double Comparatives, and Superlatives

Correct	Incorrect
1	2
3	4
6	5
	7
	8

TOTALS: 10   26

To obtain 1,027 pieces, the rope is cut 1,026 times. The 1,026th cut produces the 1,027th piece.

2-53 As Easy as Pie: Comparisons with *As*

1. Gloria isn't as *hungry* as Mr. Jones. **or** Gloria is as hungry as Mr. Jones.
Mr. Jones isn't as *young* as Gloria.
Gloria isn't as *old* as Mr. Jones.

2. Nerd's nose isn't as *long* as Nerda's.
Nerda's nose isn't as *short* as Nerd's.
Nerd's nose is nearly as *long* as Nerda's.

3. Olaf isn't as *alert* as George.
George isn't as *sleepy* as Olaf.

2-54 A Sitting Duck: Present Participles as Adjectives

1. bowling
2. diving
3. frightening
4. speeding
5. weeping
6. flying
7. sitting
8. laughing

2-55 The Two-Headed Man: Noun Plus *ed* as Adjective

2. Horned woman
3. Open-mouthed bird
4. Bandaged man
5. Bearded man
6. Long-haired woman
7. Hook-nosed woman (**or** man **or** person) or long-nosed woman (**or** man **or** person)
8. Double-chinned man

2-56 A Worried Mom: More Noun-Plus-*ed* Adjectives

1. Long-necked woman
2. Long-tongued man
3. One-legged bird
4. Long-eared dog
5. Boxed fox
6. Wrecked car
7. Caged bird
8. Striped shirt

2-57 A Broken Heart: Past Participles as Adjectives

A. E
B. T
C. I
D. W
E. C
F. O
G. L
H. D
I. S
J. A

Cryptogram: *Twice Told Tales*

2-58 Who Came Lately: Adjectives and Adverbs

2. He/She writes well.
3. He/She speaks intelligently.
4. He/She laughs happily.
5. He speaks wisely.
6. He/She speaks interestingly.
7. He/She works hard.
8. He/She rises early.
9. He/She gets to class late.
10. He/She walks heavily.
11. You walk far.
12. He/She speaks wittily.

2-59 Who Drives "Fastlier": Comparison of Adverbs

1. A
2. E
3. F
4. H
5. I
6. L
7. N
8. O
9. R
10. S
11. T
12. X

ONE HALF + THREE SIXTHS = 1

2-60   Dad Is Tied Up at the Office: Present, Past Passive

T	E	A
E	A	T
A	T	E

The idiom "tied up" means delayed or detained. Dad cannot leave the office because he is busy.

2-61   By and By: The Use of *By* in the Passive

2. The bridge was built in 1990.
3. Corn is grown in the Midwest.
4. *Romeo and Juliet* was written by William Shakespeare.
5. The electric light bulb was invented by Thomas Edison.
6. My portable cassette player was stolen at the beach.
7. The package was delivered at 6:00.
8. The speech was delivered by the President.
9. Our house was built in 1985.
10. This house was designed by my grandfather.

2-62 He'll Be Spread Too Thin: Future and Present Perfect Passive

2. A lot of fish will probably be caught.
3. The enemy camp is going to be surrounded.
4. The criminals have been arrested.
5. Two senators from each state are going to be elected.
6. The lights have been fixed.
7. The weather report will be given at 10:00.
8. The movie is going to be reviewed.
9. The bank has been robbed.
10. The jewelry is going to be stolen.

BONUS QUESTION: If people are spread too thin, they are doing too many things at the same time. Therefore, they can really do none of them well.

2-63 I "Oughta" Go Now: Modal Auxiliaries

1. 7 Y
2. 1 O
3. 4 U
4. 11 T
5. 3 U
6. 9 R
7. 2 N
8. 8 M
9. 10 E
10. 5 O
11. 6 N

ANSWER TO RIDDLE: You turn me on.

BONUS QUESTION: "You turn me on" means "I like you very much."

2-64 He Must Have Forgotten: Three Uses of *Must*

1. M
2. U
3. S
4. T
5. H
6. A
7. V
8. E
9. L
10. O
11. S
12. T

Answer: He must have lost the phone number.

2-65 If the Cat's Away, the Mice Will Play: Present-Future Conditional Pattern

Answers will vary.

2-66 A Land of Milk and Honey: More Conditional Patterns

Answers will vary.

2-67 Which Doctor?: Conditional Review

1. C
2. D
3. E
4. H
5. I
6. K
7. O
8. R
9. S
10. T

Answer: THE SICK DOCTOR

BONUS QUESTION: The sick doctor takes care of the well one.

2-68 Pie in the Sky: Present Wishes

1. Tadeusz wishes he could speak English well.
2. I wish I didn't have lots of problems.
3. I wish I danced well.
4. I wish I didn't cry easily.
5. Yuko and Yoko wish they didn't look alike.
6. Slim wishes he weren't tall and thin.
7. Slim wishes he had a Jaguar.
8. Boris wishes he didn't have a bad complexion.
9. Tod wishes he got high grades.
10. Li wishes he could visit Taipei this summer.
11. Natasha wishes she could get a date with Gregor.
12. Mr. and Mrs. Sikand wish they owned their own home.

BONUS QUESTION: Something you want that is easily available in your dreams.

2-69 A Few Dollars and a Little Cash: Count and Non-Count Nouns

Money	*Dollar*	*Dollars*	*Furniture*
The	A	The	The
Some	The	Several	Some
A lot of		Some	A lot of
A little		Two	A little
Much		A few	Much
		A lot of	
		Many	

Chair	*Chairs*	*Apple*	*Apples*
A	The	A	The
The	Several	The	Several
	Some		Some
	Two		Two
	A few		A few
	A lot of		A lot of
	Many		Many

Things	*Stuff*	*Salt*	*Jewelry*
The	The	The	The
Several	Some	Some	Some
Some	A lot of	A lot of	A lot of
Two	A little	A little	A little
A few	Much	Much	Much
A lot of			
Many			

3-1 Ouch: One-Word Sentences

A. Ugh; Ick
B. Wow
C. Whoopee
D. Oh; Oops; Whoops
E. Ouch; Ow
F. Darn, Heck; Oops; Whoops

3-2 Love Him or Leave Him: Imperative Sentences

Note: Students may use different verbs and still be correct. Allow for these differences, as long as their choices make sense.

1. Hurry
2. Enjoy
3. Wind (or Watch)
4. Close
5. Mind
6. Take
7. Hang
8. Hold
9. Wait
10. Follow (or Watch)
11. Tie
12. Wash
13. Watch
14. Be
15. Beware
16. Open
17. Do
18. Read
19. Love
20. Be
21. Eat
22. Have
23. Leave
24. Don't be
25. Stop

3-3 The Hyena Laughed: Subject and Verb Sentences

Present progressive is used in the answers, although other tenses are acceptable.

1. Gregor is yawning.
2. George is dreaming.
3. Yuko is standing.
4. Natasha is crying.
5. Tadeusz is frowning.
6. Hans and Boris are laughing.

3-4 The Cat Is Fat: Subject, Be, Adjective

Note: Students' sentences may vary.

1. The hat is flat.
   The hat is round.
2. Rick is sick.
   Rick is ill.
3. The owl is wise.
   The owl is thoughtful.
4. Nerd is silly.
   Nerd is foolish.
5. Morton is sloppy.
   Morton is untidy.
6. The creature is strange.
   The creature is odd.

3-5 Mo is a Monster: Subject, Be, Noun

1. Ho Buom, Slim, and Stacy are friends.
2. Ice hockey is a sport.
3. The king is a coward.
4. The floor is a door.
5. The hat is a bat.
6. Coins are money.
7. A cat is a pet.

3-6 Magic Wheel: Subject, Verb, Object Sentences

Answers will vary.

3-7 They Fight at Night: Subject, Verb, Phrase

Note: Students' sentences may vary from these samples.

1. Slim is sitting beside Stacy.
2. Slim is dreaming about a Jaguar.
3. The horse is sitting on a rocking chair.
4. The cow jumped over the moon.
5. Money grows on trees.

3-8 A Girl and a Car: Subject, Verb, Object, Adjectival Modifier

Answers will vary.

3-9 Mad Mary Drove Her Car Into a Brick Wall: Subject, Verb, Object, Adverbial Modifier

1. (f)uriously; down the (a)venue
2. (s)lowly; in his mou(th)

3. (w)ildly
4. in the icy str(ee)t
5. beautifu(ll)y
6. (none)
7. on his el(b)ow

8. on the (l)eg
9. (a)t her baby brother
10. so(ft)y
11. in the (e)vening

12. (h)ardly
13. in the (a)fternoon
14. to (R)andy
15. (none)
16. at (d)awn

Four adverbs that do not end in *ly:* FAST, WELL, LATE, HARD

3-10 Here and There: Verb-Subject Word Order

Simple subjects

1. rhino
2. ape
3. lion
4. gorilla
5. orangutang
6. giraffe
7. peacocks
8. raccoons
9. bears
10. reptiles
11. seals
12. grasshoppers
13. rose
14. eagles
15. orchids
16. monkeys
17. hippos
18. antelope

¹R	O	S	²A				
			³L	I			
			⁴G	E	⁵O	R	⁶G	E
		⁷P	E	D	⁸R	O	
			⁹B	O	¹⁰I		¹¹S
	¹²G	¹³R	¹⁴E	G	¹⁵O	R	
	¹⁶M	A	S	H	¹⁷A	¹⁸A	

3-11 I Gave My Mother to the Pencil: Indirect Objects

2. I bought my baby sister a balloon.
3. Slim gave flowers to Stacy.
4. I gave Gregor the tomatoes.
5. Slim threw Tod the basketball.
6. Mrs. Yamamoto made us supper.
7. Mr. Sikand teaches algebra to us.
8. Ranjana showed her sari to us.
9. Mrs. Rodriguez made enchiladas for us.
10. Mr. and Mrs. Kim bought dinner for us.
11. I bought a Mother's Day present for my mom.
12. Mr. Lopez told us a story about his childhood in Spain.
13. Mr. and Mrs. Sato made Christmas tree ornaments for us out of origami paper.
14. Hans built his little brother a house of cards.

3-12 I'd Rather Give Than Take: More Practice with Indirect Objects

1. I   GIVE
2. A   GAVE
3. V   GATE
4. T   TATE
5. G   TAKE
6. T
7. T
8. K

3-13 I'd Rather Have a Cola: Expressing Preference

Alternative preferences are acceptable.

1. I'd rather go out with Mo than Zo.
2. I like Nerda better than Polly.
3. I prefer pecan pie to lemon meringue pie.
4. I would rather go to New York than to the Colorado Rockies.
5. I prefer archery to bowling.

3-14 The Most Important Person in the World: Tag Questions with Auxiliaries

287

3-15 Me, Too: Affirmative Agreement

1. The dog was, too. **Or** So was the dog.
2. Gloria can, too. **Or** So can Gloria.
3. George does, too. **Or** So does George.
4. Slim and Stacy did, too. **Or** So did Slim and Stacy.

3-16 Count Me In: More Affirmative Agreement

1. Yuko does, too. **Or** So does Yuko.
2. Yoko will, too. **Or** So will Yoko.
3. George is, too. **Or** So is George.
4. Jose has, too. **Or** So has Jose.

3-17 Me Neither: Negative Agreement

[1][8] A	M		[10] O	[9] N		
[9] N		[7] I	[4] F		[2] D	
	[1] A	[12] S		[5] G	[10] O	
[7] I	[3] T		[9] N			
[9] N		[12] S	[10] O		[10] O	[6] H
					[14] W	[3] E
[10] O	[4] F		[10] O	[11] R		
[15] X			[16] Z		[8] M	[3] E

3-18 You're Not Going to Buy That Hat, Are You?: More Negative Agreement

1. T   HATE
2. V   HAVE
3. A   HOVE*
4. O   LOVE
5. H
6. L

Hove is past and past participle of *heave,* used nautically.

3-19 Bow-Wow: Embedded Questions

1. S
2. F
3. W
4. A
5. O
6. B
7. N
8. V

American dogs say: Bow-wow or woof-woof
Chinese and Japanese dogs say: wan-wan
German dogs say: vow-vow
Russian dogs say: vas-vas

Hasook's answer: "I don't know if I'll marry you."

3-20 He's Too Sick to Go to School: *Too* and *Enough* with Infinitives

2. That suitcase isn't light enough for me to carry.
3. It isn't early enough for us to go to the football game.
4. He isn't tall enough to play basketball.
5. I'm not strong enough to lift a 100-pound weight.
6. She isn't thin enough to wear tight jeans.
7. It isn't warm/hot enough for us to go swimming.
8. Her grades aren't high enough for her to get on the honor roll.
9. His vision isn't good enough for him to become a pilot.
10. He isn't happy enough to enjoy school life.
11. He isn't responsible enough to care for a pet.

3-21 He Made Me Do It: Causatives—*Make, Get*

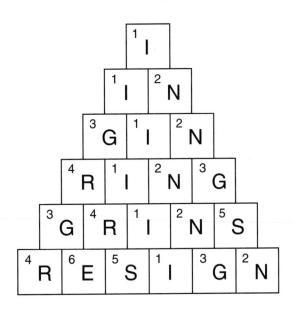

3-22   Let Me Be: Causatives—*Have, Let*

Incorrect sentences

* The cruel stepmother had Cinderella to scrub the floors all day.
          1   2
* Mother had all the windows washing.
      3   4
* The teacher let the children to run around in the kindergarten room.
              5   6   7
* Mr. Parker had us to do somersaults in gym.
      9   8
* My uncle had the broken window to repaired.
   12   11   10

Answer to riddle: The ice might *crack up*!

BONUS QUESTION: The expression *crack up* means laugh.
The activity title, "Let Me Be," is an imperative causative sentence with the subject, you, understood. "Let me be" means "Leave me alone" or "Don't bother me."

3-23   What's His Name?: Noun Clauses as Subjects

1. A
2. D
3. H
4. L
5. O
6. S
7. T
8. U
9. W
10. Y

Elephant's name: *What would you say* is that big beast's name!

3-24   I Don't Know Why I Love You: Noun Clauses as Objects

	Objects	Subjects
A	5	
B	4	
C	3	
D		10
E		7
F	1	
G	5	
H	2	
I		4
J	1	
TOTALS:	21	21

3-25 I Think So: *So* Replacing Noun Clauses

2. I think that owls are wise.
3. I think that parrots understand what you say.
4. I think that George knows the answer to the question.
5. I think that people imagine flying saucers.
6. I think that Katya is crying because Tadeusz went away.

3-26 Out of This World: Compound Sentences

1. A
2. C
3. E
4. F
5. G
6. I
7. L
8. M
9. N
10. O
11. R
12. S
13. U
14. Y

Answer to riddle: From a flying saucer

3-27 Slim's Tall, But Stacy Isn't: Compound Sentences—Reversals

Students will use different names to fill in these blanks.

2. but _____ does
3. but _____ doesn't
4. but _____ does
5. but _____ won't
6. but _____ will
7. but _____ can
8. but _____ doesn't
9. but _____ hasn't
10. but _____ didn't
11. but _____ doesn't
12. but _____ doesn't
13. but _____ is
14. but _____ does
15. but _____ has
16. but _____ won't
17. but _____ will
18. but _____ is
19. but _____ do
20. but _____ is
21. but _____ could
22. but _____ isn't

Until You Came: Complex Sentences—Subordinating Conjunctions

```
                 ¹A                          ²U
                  F              ³W  H  E  N  N
      ⁴A  L  T  H  O  U  G  H    H           T
       S           E           ⁵I           I
       S           R            L           L
       O                        E
       O       ⁶B
     ⁷U  N  L  E  S  S
       A           F
       S           O
                   R
                   E
```

3-29 The Wonderful World of the Future: Complex Sentences—Present-Future Pattern

3.   When I get married, I'm going to have two children.
4.   I'm going to have two children when I get married.
5.   Answers will vary.
6.   Answers will vary.
7.   If I meet a perfect guy/girl, I will probably go steady for awhile.
8.   I will probably go steady for awhile if I meet a perfect guy/girl.
9-22.   Answers will vary.

3-30 Which Comes First?: Complex Sentences with Time Clauses

1st	2nd
1	2
3	5
4	6
8	7
9	10

$\underline{25} \times \underline{30} = 750$

3-31 I'd Really Like to: Complex Sentences with Incomplete Infinitives

1. hatched
2. count
3. before
4. chickens
5. don't
6. your
7. are
8. they

Proverb: Don't count your chickens before they are hatched!
Meaning: Don't spend money before you earn it!

3-32 Lila Has a Car: Complex Sentences with Adjective Clauses

Answers will vary.

3-33 A Sad Cat: Complex Sentences with Medial Adjective Clauses

2. The car that Lila drove was a convertible.
3. The girl that Boris looked at was cute.
4. The soup that Murad ordered had a fly in it.
5. The fish that Gloria caught was enormous.
6. The student who had a pile of books on his desk worried about the test.
7. The blouse that Yelina liked to wear had a dollar collar.

3-34 Do We Really Want *That*?: Complex Sentences— The Use of *That* in Adjective Clauses

Correct sentences

B
E
F
I
J
M
N

1 T	2 H	3 E	4 S	5 E
6 H				7 R
8 O	9 T	10 H	11 E	12 R
13 S				14 O
15 E	16 D	17 G	18 A	19 R

3-35 Why Is Leona's Hair Standing on End?: Complex Sentences—*Because*

Answers may vary slightly.

1. Pedro is perspiring because he is hot.
2. Gloria is drinking cola because she is thirsty.
3. Olaf is tangled up in the net because he is clumsy.
4. The king is hiding behind the throne because he is afraid.
5. Nerd is putting his foot in his mouth because he is stupid.
6. Leona's hair is standing on end because she is afraid.

3-36 "Don't Buy That Tie": Reported Speech—*Not* Plus Infinitive

2. I told my father not to buy that tie.
3. I begged the hunter not to shoot the fox.
4. I told the cashier not to give me a lot of pennies.
5. The letter carrier told me not to forget the stamps.
6. I told Kahled not to hit his finger with the hammer.
7. Leona told her baby brother not to get in her hair.
8. Boris's mother told him not to fall.

3-37 "I'm Drowning": Reported Speech—Present Tense

2. Yuko said (that) she thought that dress was cute.
   Yoko said (that) she liked it, too.
3. Slim said (that) he was broke.
4. Gregor said (that) he was going to turn a somersault.
5. Emilio said (that) he didn't want any pizza.
6. Boris said (that) he didn't feel well.
7. Arthur said (that) there was a fly in his soup.

3-38 "I Cried Last Night": Reported Speech—Past Tense

1. Slim said (that) he had studied until 2:00 A.M.
2. The woodpecker said (that) he had drilled a hole in the tree.
3. Mr. Jones said (that) he had had a great dinner.
4. Bo said (that) he had pulled up a telephone pole.
5. Funny Bunny said (that) he hadn't heard me.
6. The octopus said (that) he had eaten a hamburger.
7. The ice mice said (that) they had been cold.

3-39 "I Won't Hurt You": Reported Speech—Future Tense

1. The plumber said (that) she would fix my/our leaking pipe.
2. Big Hunk said (that) we would win the game.
3. Masha said (that) she would land safely.
4. Tadeusz said (that) he would hit a homer.
5. Gregor and Natasha said (that) they would dance until dawn.
6. The astronaut said (that) he would walk on the moon.
7. Gretchen said (that) she would take a good picture of me.

3-40 "That's Silly": Reported Speech—Assorted Tenses

Part I:
1. A
2. D
3. E
4. N
5. O
6. P
7. S
8. T
9. U
10. Y

Words describing something silly: DOPEY, SAPPY, NUTTY

Part II
1. Stacy said (that) money didn't grow on trees.
2. Murad said (that) he had to hit the books.

4-1 Red Head /ĕ/: Sounds and Symbols

1. /ē/		21. /ō/	
2. /ē/, /ē/		22. /ĕ/	
3. /ĕ/		23. /ī/	
4. /ī/		24. /ē/	
5. /ō/		25. /ou/	
6. /ā/		26. /ĭ/, /ĕ/	
7. /ĕ/		27. /ou/	
8. /ī/		28. /ē/	
9. /ă/		29. /ē/	
10. /ā/		30. /ē/	
11. /ā/		31. /o͞o/	
12. /ă/		32. /ā/	
13. /ō/		33. /ē/, /ē/	
14. /ē/		34. /o͞o/	
15. /ā/		35. /o͞o/	
16. /ē/		36. /o͝o/	
17. /ī/		37. /ō/	
18. /ō/		38. /ī/	
19. /o͞o/		39. /ō/	
20. /ī/		40. /o͝o/	

4-2   A Bad Bed: Short /ă/ and /ĕ/

Answers will vary depending upon which word in each pair the teacher chooses to read.

4-3   A Bat in a Vat: /b/ and /v/

Answers will vary depending upon which word in each pair the teacher chooses to read.

4-4   I Hope You Enjoy Your Flight: /l/ and /r/

    A. lip
    B. flight
    C. flute
    D. rip
    E. fruit
    F. fright

4-5   Mr. Schick Is Very Sick: *si* and *shi*

Answers will vary depending upon which word in each pair the teacher chooses to read.

4-6   Some Thumb: /s/ and /th/

Answers will vary depending upon which word in each pair the teacher chooses to read.

4-7   Two Mouths, Two Teeth: /th/ and /*th*/

/th/ *as in think*	/*th*/ *as in they*
T	T
H	H
O	E
U	I
S	R
A	
N	W
D	E
	A
S	T
O	H
U	E
T	R
H	

4-8 "The Rain in Spain Falls Mainly in the Plain": Long /ā/

T	A	T	M	H	T	H	E	H	F
H	N	O	R	A	I	N	B	A	R
E	T	F	A	T	T	E	O	B	E
Y	E	A	O	E	O	I	U	I	I
I	P	T	P	I	C	G	Q	T	G
T	A	E	E	T	A	H	U	M	H
S	S	K	N	G	B	B	E	A	T
L	A	B	O	R	L	O	T	N	O
I	V	O	H	A	E	R	E	Y	E
H	E	A	E	Y	A	S	A	P	E

A. rain
B. skate
C. freight (train)
D. ape
E. baseball

4-9 The Many Faces of Eve: Long /ē/

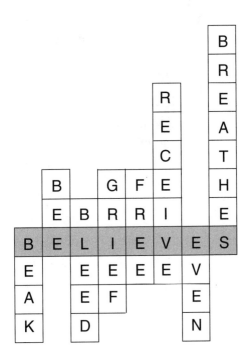

297

4-10 Our Team's Ahead: Long and Short /e/ sounds

/e/ head	/e/ eat
B	P
R	E
E	A
A	N
K	U
F	T
A	S
S	
T	

4-11 Hi, I Want to Buy a Tie: Long /ī/

1. my (m," y)
2. sigh or sight (<u>sigh,"</u> Tom)
3. buy (<u>Abu Y</u>emen)
4. lie (Al<u>l I</u> ever)
5. five (I<u>f I've</u>)
6. kite (crac<u>k it</u> even)
7. kind (Dic<u>k indi</u>cated)
8. bike (ro<u>b, I keep</u>)
9. dye (Davi<u>d, Ye</u>lina)
10. item (<u>it e</u>merged)
11. hi (<u>hi</u>s)
12. rhyme (M<u>r. Hym e</u>ats)
13. fire (<u>if I</u> reserve)
14. ice (<u>I c</u>entered)
15. mind (Ji<u>m, Indi</u>ans)

A. ti(e)
B. g(uy)
C. fr(y)
D. p(ie) in the sk(y)
E. (I)ce m(i)ce

298

4-12 Hello, Joe, What Do You Know?: Long /ō/

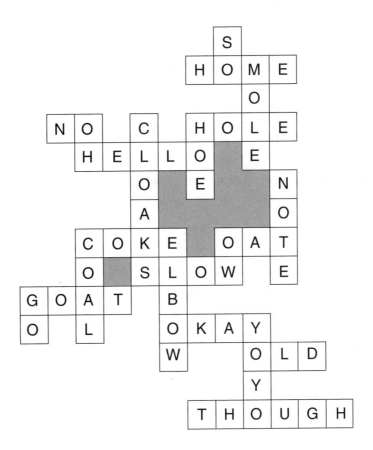

4-13 Do You Know Joe Blow?: *Ow* as in Long /ō/

1. know, Blow
2. crows, slowly, yellow
3. —
4. low
5. grow, shadows, snow
6. —
7. grown, known, mown
8. bow (a pretty bow)
9. rows (sit in rows)
10. throw, snow, know

A. glows
B. bowling
C. rowing
D. throw
E. bow

4-14 A Brown Owl: *Ow* as /ou/ or /ō/

/ou/ cow	/o/ blow
1	2
4	3
5	7
10	8
	9
	11

TOTALS: <u>20</u>   <u>40</u>

4-15 Mr. Brown Went to Town: The Sounds of *Ow* and *Ou*

1. now, cow
2. out, plow
3. flowers
4. about, Stout
5. out, without
6. Brown, town, flowered, gown
7. shout
8. frowned
9. howling, growling
10. towels
11. scowling
12. south, mouth, house
13. bough
14. allows, powder
15. how
16. owl, fowl
17. clown, down, crowd
18. —
19. Meow, Bow wow, now
20. about

4-16 He Can't Get His Foot in the Boot: Long and Short /oo/

/o͞o/ boot	/o͝o/ book
1. too	1. good
2. hoof (or o͝o)	2. stood
3. roof (or o͝o)	3. wood
4. cool	4. shook
5. pool	5. foot
6. stool	6. look
7. spool	7. brook
8. food	8. crook
9. toot-toot	9. wool
10. bloom	10. hook
11. boom	11. understood
12. broom	12. crooked
13. poor	13. took
14. spoon	14. nook
15. moon	15. cook
16. noon	

4-17 Rice Is Nice: Soft *c* Sound /s/

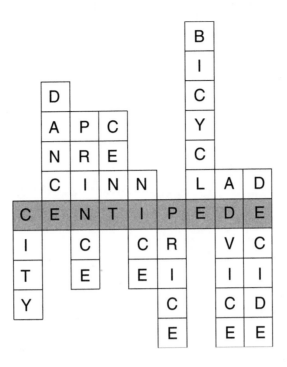

4-18 Carl Can't Come: Hard *c* Sound /k/

5. W
9. R
13. O
17. N
20. G

4-19 Get Some Knowledge in College: Soft and Hard *G* Sounds

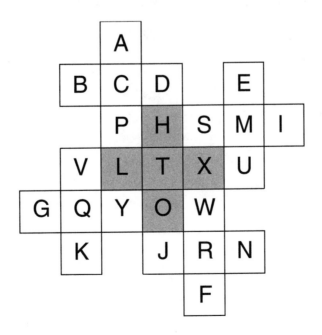

4-20   A Bear in the Air: *R*-controlled Vowels

A. *Are*
1. caviar
2. far
3. jar
4. star

B. *air*
1. care
2. rare
3. their
4. there
5. they're
6. where

C. *here*
1. dear
2. deer
3. near
4. pier
5. we're

D. *or*
1. floor
2. roar
3. store
4. tore

E. *fur*
1. purr
2. sir
3. were

4-21   A Ghastly Ghost: Silent Letters

Circled letters	Words	Silent letters
1. g	wron(g)	w
2. h	t(h)ough	g, h
3. o	g(o)at	a
4. s	(s)oap	a
5. t	kno(t)	k
6. g	knowin(g)	k
7. n	p(n)eumonia	p
8. o	n(o)te	e
9. m	(m)ean	a
10. e	receiv(e)	i

4-22 "It's Rough," She Said with a Cough as She Sat on the Bough: Like and Unlike Pronunciations

Same	Different
C	A
E	B
F	D
G	H
I	J
K	L
M	Q
N	R
O	T
P	V
S	X
U	Y
<u>W</u>	<u>Z</u>
13	13

4-23 Please Sneeze: Same Pronunciation, Different Spellings

A. 23, 29, 32, 42, 50
B. 25
C. 18, 40, 46
D. 20, 30
E. 3, 45
F. 51
G. 5, 12, 15, 36, 41, 55, 56
H. 4, 35, 49, 58
I. 39, 47
J. 14
K. 11
L. 10, 22, 28, 53
M. 9
N. 13, 17, 38
O. 34, 37
P. 2, 24
Q. 16, 33, 43
R. 19, 54
S. 7
T. 31, 57
U. 1, 21
V. 27
W. 26, 44, 52
X. 8
Y. 6, 48

4-24 The Rabbit Habit: A Short Vowel Pattern

```
          B  E  N  D
    B  L  A  N  K  E  T
    S  A  D  N  E  S  S
    C  A  M  E  L
       M  I  N  T
    F  A  N  T  A  S  T  I  C
 P  L  A  N  T  I  N  G
    S  H  O  P  P  I  N  G
 T  H  A  N  K
```

4-25 I Hat Your Hat: Magic *E*

1. MAT, MATE
2. PIN, PINE
3. WIN, WINE
4. FIN, FINE
5. BIT, BITE
6. CUT, CUTE
7. DIN, DINE
8. MIN, MINE
9. TIN, TINE
10. SLIM, SLIME
11. PLAN, PLANE
12. DIM, DIME
13. SCAT, SKATE

4-26 People Live Their Lives: Pronunciation of Final *S* as /s/ or /z/

Part I:

Proverb: Walls have ears.
Meaning: Be cautious when you talk about personal business. Someone might be listening.

Part II:

1. queens /z/
2. tops /s/
3. zippers /z/
4. dogs /z/

W	B	A	C	L
L	D	S	P	H
A	F	G	V	E
E	A	I	R	J
K	M	S	N	O

4-27　Huh?: /ə/ in Unaccented Syllables

1. A, about *or* I, agree
2. I, agree *or* A, about
3. K, allow
4. N, approve
5. H, awful
6. S, beautiful
7. G, comfortable
8. M, dependent
9. E, different
10. D, enemy
11. B, exercise
12. L, famous
13. J, intelligent
14. F, miserable *or* R, mister
15. F, miserable *or* R, mister
16. Q, restaurant
17. O, terrible *or* P, terrific
18. O, terrible *or* P, terrific
19. T, victory
20. C, wonderful

4-28　We Smiled, Talked, and Waited: Three Pronunciations of *ed*

/t/	/d/	/əd/
walked	rained	pounded
watched	shaved	folded
talked	killed	counted
finished	enjoyed	sorted
	showed	visited
kissed		
touched	explained	
	wanted	

Proverb: When it rains, it pours.
Meaning: Often bad things seem to happen together.

4-29 Who'll Be at the Party?: Question Words Contracted with Verbs

Though this activity can be done as a written exercise, it is useful for students to make the connection between spoken English and uncontracted meanings.

1. Where am
2. Why is
3. When is
4. Where are
5. Why are
6. How are
7. When will
8. Who will
9. What will
10. Where did
11. What did
12. How did
13. Why has
14. Where has
15. What has
16. What is
17. When is
18. How is
19. How did
20. How would
21. What have
22. Where have
23. Where have
24. How have
25. Who have

5-1 Hi, I'm Rosa: Making Friends

1. A. "Hi, I'm Toshi. What's your name?"
    B. "Hi, Toshi. I'm Gregor."
    A. "Nice to meet you, Gregor. Where are you from?"
    B. "I'm from Moscow. How about you?"
    A. "I'm from Tokyo. How do you like America?"
    B. "I think it's great. How about you?"
    A. "Me, too."

2. A. "Hi, I'm Zoa. What's your name?"
    B. "Hi, Zoa. I'm Ho Buom."
    A. "Nice to meet you, Ho Buom. Where are you from?"
    B. "I'm from Korea. How about you?"
    A. "I'm from Nigeria. How do you like America?"
    B. "I like it, but I think English is hard. How about you?"
    A. "Me, too."

5-2 How Are You Doing?: Assorted Answers

1	2	3	4	5	6	7
8	9	10	11	12	13	14
15	16	17	18	19	20	21

5-3 How About a Soda?: Making Suggestions

A. 2. How about going skating?
    3. Let's go skating.

B. 1. Why don't we have/eat a hamburger.
    2. How about a hamburger?
    3. Let's have/eat a hamburger.

C. 1. Why don't we ask Cora and Dora?
    2. How about Cora and Dora?
    3. Let's ask Cora and Dora.

D. 2. How about going to the zoo?
    3. Let's go to the zoo.

E. 2. How about a Western?
    3. Let's buy a Western.

F. 1. Why don't we get a dog?
    2. How about a dog?
    3. Let's get a dog.

5-4 Happy Talk: Looking Forward To

A   DENTAL APPOINTMENT

5-5 Over Easy: Restaurant Talk

1. C-O-R-R-E-C-T
2. O-K-A-Y
3. O-K
4. Y-E-S

5-6 How About You?: Assorted Meanings

1. A
2. B
3. E
4. F
5. K
6. L
7. O
8. P
9. R
10. U
11. Y

Proverb: Look before you leap
Meaning: Think and plan before you act. Don't act hastily.

5-7   What to Say When: Assorted Social Phrases

1. G
2. K
3. M
4. L
5. P
6. E
7. O
8. A
9. Q
10. D
11. R
12. J
13. T
14. B
15. N
16. S
17. H
18. I
19. F
20. C

5-8   I Love Your Sweater: Clothes Compliments

A.   tux you're wearing
     looks _____ (*adjectives will vary*)
     I love/like your tux.

B.   Answers will vary.

5-9   That's Very Sweet of You: Words of Praise

Answers will vary.

5-10   May I Call You Tonight?: Requests and Permission

The correct sentences are:

1. A
3. E
4. H
5. I
7. L
8. O
9. R
11. T
12. U
13. V
14. Y

Compliment: I LOVE YOUR HAT. In many languages, *love* is used to express deep feeling for a loved person, *not* for objects.

5-11   I'm Sorry, I Didn't Catch That: Asking People to Repeat

Answers may vary. These are examples:

1. I'm sorry. Could you repeat that?
2. I'm sorry. I didn't get what you said.
3. I'm sorry *or* Excuse me *or* Pardon me. Will you say that again more slowly?
4. I beg your pardon *or* I didn't catch that.
5. I'm sorry. What was that? *or* What did you say?
6. I beg your pardon. I didn't catch what you said.
7. Excuse me. I didn't quite understand what you said.
8. I beg your pardon. I didn't follow you.
9. I'm sorry. I don't understand.
10. I'm sorry. What was that? *or* What did you say?

5-12   Doing Anything Saturday Night?: Planning a Date

1.   4, 1, 6, 3, 5, 2
2.   2, 4, 5, 3, 6, 1
3.   3, 5, 2, 6, 4, 1

5-13 May I Show You a Lovely Purple and Orange Dress?: Shopping

1. B. Yes, I'm looking for a one-piece swim suit.
   B. Answers will vary.

2. B. Yes, I'm looking for a simple black dress.
   B. Answers will vary.

3. B. Yes, I'm looking for a raincoat.
   B. Answers will vary.

4. B. Yes, I'm looking for a knee-length skirt.
   B. Answers will vary.

5. B. Yes, I'm looking for a pair of comfortable low-heeled shoes.
   B. Answers will vary.

5-14 Can You Ever Forgive Me?: Apologies

Four words are: MEET, HOME, METAL, AMERICA

1. E
2. T
3. H
4. O
5. T
6. A
7. L
8. A
9. R
10. I
11. C
12. A

NOTES

DISCARD

DISCARD

ALBANY
COLLEGE OF
LIBRARY